ACKNO

I wish to thank the members of my staff, who have contributed to the publication of this book. At Barberi Law, our approach to serving our clients' legal needs is to have attorneys concentrate on work in each of the major areas of law in which our firm provides legal services. Currently, at Barberi Law our firm specializes on litigating cases in court. Our litigation cases include cases involving injuries received from a motor vehicle accident, medical malpractice, and dog bites; family law and divorce and we also provide representation to individuals in criminal justice cases. That being said, our litigation team also represents individuals involved in will contests and lawsuits involving estates, including wrongful death cases. When clients of Barberi Law are in need of estate planning or Medicaid Planning, we currently work with attorney Mark Pasquali, who is of counsel with us. Mark was also helpful in reviewing this book's section regarding Medicaid Planning. Additionally, Attorney Sara Sastamoinen, also of counsel to our firm, provided great assistance in compiling various sections of this book. Lastly, I also appreciate the numerous well-typed revisions made by my paralegal, Lori Erskin, as we edited numerous drafts of this book.

WHAT OTHERS HAVE TO SAY
ABOUT THIS BOOK

"I've known Attorney Barberi for years. He has represented clients in my court on various legal matters. This book is the most comprehensive work that I have ever read on estate planning and related subject matters. It is a treasure that every family should read before choosing an estate plan. It is obvious to me that Mr. Barberi spent hours thinking about possible problems a family might encounter when thinking about their own estate plan. I did not ask, nor did I receive, anything of value for my review for this thorough treatise!"

The Honorable Jack T. Arnold
Retired Gratiot County Probate Judge

"Once again Mr. Barberi has taken a commonly perceived complicated issue and boiled it down to the nuts and bolts of protecting your family. In my forty years of experience advising clients of the importance of estate planning, I found that it has been received as a necessary process but difficult to implement. Joe Barberi has clearly defined the benefits and presents a road map to protect your family and other loved ones in preserving assets and providing you peace of mind."

Paul B. Murray, CPA
Robert F. Murray & Company
Mount Pleasant, Midland, and Bay City, Michigan

"As an Assisted Living Community Manger I feel that the information provided throughout this book is a great tool not only for our seniors but for the children of those who have parents contemplating moving into or that are currently in a care facility. Most residents in my facility have already taken the step of having one or more of these documents drawn up but they often have not been updated to the current status of their situation. Most frequently what we experience is that neither party has an understanding as when, why or how some of these documents become activated. Very useful information for the families to share with their parents to help them understand why it's important to update those documents and also for helping the children to be sure theirs are set up correctly for their future needs. It was a great read for me, it answered some of my concerns."

Sharie Barringer
Community Manager

"You don't have to feel intimidated about estate planning issues any more. The objective of this book is to educate the reader on the many moving parts that comprise an estate plan and Joe's book accomplishes that objective. This book will give you a base understanding of what's involved in the process and what some of your potential options could be in developing an estate plan. In my opinion, estate planning is one of the most overlooked areas in a person's financial affairs but perhaps one of the most important financial task. A well drafted and executed estate plan will provide your family with peace of mind and allow you to efficiently distribute your wealth according to your wishes."

Shannon M. Astrike, CPA PFS
Founder and Principal of Astrike Financial PLLC,
an Accounting and Wealth Management
Practice in Midland, Michigan

"As normal for Joe when he does anything, Joe Barberi's book covering estate, disability and death planning is a certain success. The book covers each specific area of estate planning in a condensed yet comprehensive manner, which makes the reader's research straightforward. I know of very few people who perform as thorough research as Joe has done in this book. Well done!"

Robert Elmore
Certified Public Accountant
Mt. Pleasant, Michigan

WHAT OTHERS HAVE TO SAY ABOUT
MR. BARBERI AND HIS STAFF

Our experience at Barberi Law was excellent. After listening to our estate goals, a concrete plan was implemented to provide the best possible solution for us. I felt extremely confident in the staff at Barberi Law and would recommend anyone needing assistance with elder law issues to contact Joe's firm.

James McBryde
A satisfied Isabella County Estate Planning Client–2015

We were pleased with the way Joe helped us with our trust. He came up with a unique plan for our complicated wishes.

Dean and Judy Kreiner
Mt. Pleasant, Michigan

"When my Aunt needed nursing care, I turned to Joe Barberi's law firm and Mark Pasquali to guide us through the Medicaid policy and qualification. I was very pleased with their results and would recommend them to anyone facing the high costs of nursing care for a loved one."

Connie B.
Mt. Pleasant, Michigan

"I have known Joe Barberi many years, professionally and personally. He has written several trusts for Helen and me. Mark Pasquali has assisted him. They have always performed professionally and accurately. Joe is a good teacher and always answers all questions so that things are clearly understood. The office staff is also very thorough, helpful, and efficient. We would not hesitate to recommend this office to anyone considering trust and estate work."

Larry Leemaster
Mt. Pleasant, Michigan

"My family has been very pleased with the professional work and 'personal touches' provided by the Barberi Law firm through attorney Mark Pasquali and paralegal Julie Rademacher related to my mother's estate and her placement in a local nursing facility. Five star service and reasonable fees!"

Mark A. Cwiek
Mount Pleasant resident

ESTATE PLANNING
IN MICHIGAN

SECRETS FOR PROTECTING YOUR SAVINGS
From the High Costs of Nursing Home Care

MISTAKES
Commonly Made Trying To Avoid Probate

- Protecting Your Assets During Your Lifetime
- Planning For The Possibility of Your Disability
- Making Sure Your Assets Go Where You Want After Your Death

Attorney Joseph T. Barberi

BARBERI LAW

2305 Hawthorn Drive, Ste C,
Mt. Pleasant, MI 48858

1-800-336-3423

www.barberilawfirm.com

Printed in the United States of America.

ISBN: 978-1-63385-130-6
Library of Congress Control Number: 2016904090
$17.95

Designed and published by

Word Association Publishers
205 Fifth Avenue
Tarentum, Pennsylvania 15084

www.wordassociation.com
1.800.827.7903

CONTENTS

Introduction..1

Chapter 1   What Is Estate Planning? 5
            What Is Elder Law? 6
            The Importance of Estate Planning.................7

Chapter 2   Planning for Disability 11
            Medical Power of Attorney 13
            Choosing the Best Patient Advocate.............15
            Distribute Your Medical Power of Attorney .. 16
            It Is Never Too Soon 17
            Revocation of Medical Power of Attorney 18
            Financial Power of Attorney 19
            Effective Upon Execution or Incapacity 21
            Revocation of Power of Attorney 22
            Possible Abuse..23
            When the Court Becomes Involved:
                Conservatorship and Guardianship 24
            Conservatorship...25
            Guardianship 25

Chapter 3   Specific Goals When Planning
            for Death 27
            Expanding on Your After-Death Estate
                Planning Goals 29
            Five Common Goals that People Have When
                It Comes to Formulating an Estate Plan 30
            What Happens Without an Estate Plan? 33
            Will or Trust? 36
            The Power of Time 39
            Protecting Your Beneficiaries from
                Their Creditors 40
            The Use of Beneficiary Designations............41
            Lady Bird Deeds...42

Why You Still Need a Will
(Even with a Trust) 43
Many Different Types of Trusts 45

Chapter 4 Medicaid Planning............................47
Protecting Your Assets 49
Michigan's Estate Recovery 52
Myths 54
Nuts and Bolts of Medicaid.......................... 55
The Look Back Period 57

Chapter 5 Top Six Mistakes People Make in
Estate Planning 59
1. Taking the DIY Approach to
   Estate Planning... 59
2. Not Taking Care of Life Insurance Issues . 70
3. Choosing the Wrong Estate Planner 73
4. Waiting Until It's Too Late....................... 74
5. Not Updating Your Will or Estate Plan 76
6. Not Maximizing Your Social
   Security Benefits 76

Chapter 6 Probate and Administration Estate ...83
How Long Does Probate Take? 86
How Can a Will Be Contested? 87
A Case in Point.. 87
Trust Administration 89

Chapter 7 Special Circumstances Require
Special Planning 91
Taking Care of Loved Ones
   with Disabilities 91
Estates Subject to the Federal Estate Tax 93
Second Marriages and Blended Families....... 94
Same-Sex Couples 95

When Going Through a Divorce 99

The Role of Prenuptial and Postnuptial

Agreements in Estate Planning 102

Chapter 8 **Estate Planning Scams 107**

What Are Estate Planning Scams? 108

What Should You Look Out for? 112

What Services Can an Estate Planning Attorney

    Provide that a Non-lawyer Can't?............. 113

Chapter 9 **Eight Actions to Take Right**

Now to Preserve Your Wealth for

Your Family 115

1. Consult a Lawyer 116

2. Separate Business from

    Personal Finances 116

3. Establish Liability Insurances 117

4. Set Up Life Insurance 117

6. Utilize Retirement Accounts 118

7. Understand Your Pension 118

8. Create a Trust 119

Chapter 10 **Resources 121**

Barberi Law Free Estate Planning and

    Asset Protection Workshops 121

Barberi Law Monthly Newsletter 122

Five Wishes 122

Isabella County Commission on Aging 123

Senior Services of Midland County 123

American Association of Retired

    Persons (AARP): 124

Association of Mature American

    Citizens (AMAC):.................................. 124

Senior Times of South Central Michigan 125
Hospice and Palliative Care Association
    of Michigan 125
Michigan Funeral Directors Association
    (MFDA).. 125
Area Agencies on Aging (AAAs) 126
Get What's Yours – The Secret to Maxing
    Out Your Social Security 126

Chapter 11 Epilogue... 127
About the Author 137

INTRODUCTION

Situations like the cases I refer to in this book are some of the reasons I have written this book. I hope that you, the reader, can appreciate that sometimes having a little knowledge can be dangerous. Yes, it's good to know about wills, powers of attorney, and trusts and some of the different things they can accomplish and prevent. And yes, I am aware that in the Internet-driven world in which we live, there are websites—such as LegalZoom, Rocket Lawyer, and Nolo—that, for a small fee, can give the user access to boilerplate forms designed to accomplish a certain level of estate planning. No doubt, spending $19.95 to download a will might seem attractive to the user rather than paying a lawyer $350 to draft a unique will (fact specific to the client).

That being said, when drafting a will, any lawyer worth his or her salt would strongly suggest that the individual also create powers of attorney at the same time and, while talking with the client, the lawyer also would likely inquire as to how the client's assets are currently titled. For example, the attorney may ask questions such as the following: Do you own any real estate? If so, what is on your deed? What about any checking or savings accounts, and how are they titled? Do you have any deferred compensation accounts? Are there beneficiaries named for any deferred compensation accounts? Do you own any stocks and, if so, are there any transfer-on-death (TODs) designations in place? Do you have life insurance, and if so, who are your beneficiaries?

After learning the answers to such basic planning questions, the estate planning attorney would then typically discuss planning options available to the individual, including the possibility of the utilization of a trust to best accomplish the client's goals. And, plans should also be made for what the client would like to have happen if he or she becomes disabled (e.g., Would the client prefer to be cared for at home or in an assisted living facility?). This process of talking with an experienced estate planner cannot be accomplished by downloading boilerplate forms off the Internet. And when disability strikes, or as the case may be, death, it is invaluable to have a trusted estate planning attorney or members of his or her law firm available to answer questions for family members. Again, these discussions and ongoing personalized advice cannot be obtained by "Googling" questions.

So, with the caveat that "a little knowledge can be dangerous," you are encouraged to review the information provided in this book to raise your awareness of estate planning, probate and Medicaid issues that should be addressed and acted upon by you, well before your disability or death. After reviewing the material in this book, it is my hope that you will possess the knowledge necessary to meet with an estate-planning attorney to intelligently discuss creating your unique estate plan.

CHAPTER 1

WHAT IS ESTATE PLANNING?

An estate plan is simply a set of written instructions that you create for others and your loved ones so that everyone knows how you want to be cared for if you become disabled. It also lists your wishes regarding the distribution of your assets after your death. Estate planning includes compiling important documentation and engaging in the proper titling of your assets to accomplish your wishes for asset distribution, as part of your estate, or by direct transfer after your death to designated beneficiaries. A comprehensive estate plan includes a will, a trust(s), powers of attorney, advance health care directives, and, typically, after-death instructions (plans for a funeral and/or cremation).

I understand that individuals can feel uneasy when talking about estate plans and considering other issues that arise with advanced age. I recognize that thinking about the care you will receive and the way your hard-earned assets will be distributed after death can be emotional and troubling. With this in mind, our estate planning and elder law legal team at Barberi Law does everything possible to make it easy for our clients to develop sound estate and care plans and to minimize the stress and discomfort that can come with the planning process.

WHAT IS ELDER LAW?
You may have heard or read the phrase "elder law" and wondered what it meant and if it differs from estate planning. Elder law is an interdisciplinary field of law that addresses the needs of seniors, people with disabilities, and those conducting end-of-life planning at any stage of their lives. It typically encompasses issues related to finances, health care, and asset distribution. Our elder law team at Barberi Law possesses a vast knowledge regarding a myriad of ancillary issues that encompass the term "elder law." Such issues include

- wills and trusts;
- Medicaid planning;
- long-term care and Medicaid eligibility;
- planning for incapacity;
- nursing home issues;
- asset protection;
- guardianships or conservatorships;

- powers of attorney;
- advance directives;
- social security and other income-related matters;
- probate;
- eligibility for veteran's benefits; and
- after-death instructions regarding funeral or cremation issues.

> *"Elder law" addresses the needs of seniors, people with disabilities, and those conducting end-of-life planning at any stage of their lives.*

Many of these topics can affect a person's life at any age. You do not have to be considered "elderly" to take advantage of the many benefits of elder law planning.

THE IMPORTANCE OF ESTATE PLANNING

Estate planning is one of those things in life that most of us have good intentions of doing but never seem to get around to accomplishing. Or, it seems too daunting a task to take on, or you don't know where to start. Or, you're a young parent or someone with few assets, and you think that you don't need an estate plan. Or, it seems too expensive. Or, you're afraid that by writing your will, it will somehow speed up or cause your death.

Sadly, there are countless examples of people who were going to get around to estate planning, thought it was too complicated, thought it was too expensive, thought they were too young to worry about it, or had relatively few assets who very much needed an estate plan. But, because they didn't have one, their loved ones suffered, financially and emotionally. I'm sure you know of someone who died as a young parent, leaving one or more minor children behind and possibly a spouse. I'm sure you know of someone, who, after her parents died, became engaged in disputes with her siblings about dividing mom and dad's "stuff." I'm sure you know of someone, who despite seeming to have only a few assets, left behind messy financial matters for his loved ones to resolve after his death. I'm sure you know of someone who was in the situation of having to decide whether to "pull the plug" on a loved one. These are all situations when having an estate plan would have been extremely valuable and helpful for all involved. I will explain in later chapters how each facet of an estate plan works and how it serves the person who created it and their loved ones.

Estate planning is not just for you; it is also for your family. It is a gift you give to them. You are giving them the peace of mind of knowing what, when, where, and how to take action if you are ill or incapacitated and what you want them to do after your death. You are saving them money and preserving family relationships. You are ensuring that you financially provide for your family in the best way you can after your death. Accordingly, as stated, estate planning truly is a gift, and I encourage you to think of it in that way—it's your gift to your family.

At the outset of this book, you may not know what estate planning means and all that it encompasses, and you may be unsure of how having an estate plan will benefit you, personally. Specifically, when you think of estate planning, some of these questions may come to mind:

- Do I need both a will and a trust?
- What assets are covered in a simple will?
- What is probate?
- What documents comprise a comprehensive estate plan?

Continue to read on, as I address and provide answers to each of these questions and more.

CHAPTER 2

PLANNING FOR DISABILITY

When we think of estate planning, most of us think of wills and how our assets will be distributed after our deaths. But, in my opinion, what is even more important than planning for our deaths is planning for our disability. There is a significant chance that at some point in our lives, we will come to be in a physical and/or mental state when we cannot make or communicate our wishes for health care or handle our own financial matters. To that end, we need to ensure that we plan properly for our potential disability.

All comprehensive estate plans should include written documents that spell out how you want to be cared for and who you choose to act on your behalf in the event that you become legally incapacitated. You may find yourself in such a situation due to illness, degenerative diseases, traumatic accidents, coma, stroke, Alzheimer's disease, dementia or other neurological impairment, or any number of causes.

There are two primary resources estates planners use to help clients plan for disability: powers of attorney for health care, including a patient advocate designation, and powers of attorney for financial matters. These are both documents that are created as part of overall estate plans, although they each can be created on their own. Often, when my divorce clients first come to see me, I advise them to create or revise their powers of attorney but not their overall estate plan at that time. These two powers of attorney documents spell out directions about what should be done in certain circumstances and also appoint one or more individual(s) to act in the person's behalf when the person is unable to and, in certain circumstances, as a matter of convenience. In addition to powers of attorney, estate planners who create trusts for their clients can draft trust agreements to govern the management of trust assets during a person's incapacity.

Under Michigan law, a power of attorney can be made "durable," which is a legal term of art, by including words in the power of attorney to the effect that the power continues irrespective of the grantor's physical or mental incapacitation. When such language is included within the power of attorney, the power of attorney is said to be durable. Throughout this section, when I refer to a power of attorney, I mean a durable power of attorney.

Two primary resources estates planners use to help clients plan for disability are medical powers of attorney, including a patient advocate designation, and financial powers of attorney.

MEDICAL POWER OF ATTORNEY

In Michigan, creating a power of attorney for health care, commonly known as a medical directive and patient advocate designation, is a vital part of estate planning. A medical directive is a document in which you spell out in detail any wishes for medical care and appoint another person to carry out those wishes in the event that you become unable to act on your behalf. In Michigan, the person appointed is known as the "patient advocate." In short, a medical directive allows you to remain in control of your own medical treatment, even when you are physically or mentally no longer able to do so. You may become unable to participate in medical decision-making due to any number of conditions or diseases, such as Alzheimer's, dementia, brain injuries, or complications following a stroke. In somewhat crass terms, medical powers of attorney are often known as "pull-the-plug" documents in which you lay out the terms under which you want life-sustaining treatments to stop. Do Not Resuscitate (DNR) documents are similar to medical powers of attorney. If you give permission to your patient advocate in your medical power of attorney to execute a DNR on your behalf, your advocate will be able to do so if presented a DNR by a medical provider. Often in situations when hospice care is involved, health care providers seek out the signature on DNRs to save patients from traumatizing and often needless life-saving measures such as cardiopulmonary resuscitation (CPR).

The medical directive makes others aware of the kind of medical treatment you want and in what situations. For example, as a patient you can describe your wishes about whether you want to be cared for in a nursing home, to receive palliative care, or to donate your organs. A medical power of attorney also spells out how your physical needs are to be addressed and what activities you want to engage in, if possible, including where you wish to reside during any period of incapacity. You may want to describe the types of food you prefer to eat, the traditions you like to celebrate, and the events in which you like to participate (such as deer hunting or football games). More notably, you let your patient advocate know what to do in the event of any condition in which only life support is keeping you alive and you are in a persistent vegetative state or not expected to live once life support efforts (for example, a ventilator or intubation) are discontinued. Generally, a medical directive will only be effective after (1) it is signed by the patient, (2) the patient advocate signs a standard acceptance form, (3) it is given to the patient's health care provider for inclusion in the patient's medical records, and (4) the patient's physician and another physician or psychologist state in writing that the patient is unable to participate in making medical decisions.

CHOOSING THE BEST PATIENT ADVOCATE

One of the most important features of a medical power of attorney is the patient advocate designation. Choosing someone to carry out your wishes for medical care is a very weighty decision. As stated, the person you select to carry out your medical treatment decisions is called a patient advocate. Your medical power of attorney is your patient advocate's instructions about how decisions should be made and gives your patient advocate the ability and the duty to carry out those instructions.

Ideally, you should appoint an advocate in whom you have great confidence, you believe has good judgment, and you believe will follow your written directives that you have included in your specific medical power of attorney. This person should be easy to reach in an emergency and, therefore, should live near you and, most importantly, would be able to make a decision that could end your life. It is also wise to appoint successor patient advocates to act on your behalf in the event that your first choice for a patient advocate is unavailable or otherwise unable to act.

Again, ideally, your chosen patient advocate should live geographically close to you and be readily available to meet with doctors and medical professionals at any time. Your patient advocate should be able to be there quickly in case of an emergency. I never recommend that you appoint relatives who reside in a different state or country from you, no matter how much you trust them. Even with phone, e-mail, and other ways to communicate now, being unable to be physically present to assess a situation can put major restrictions on a person's ability to make good medical choices for you.

DISTRIBUTE YOUR MEDICAL POWER OF ATTORNEY

After you have properly executed your medical power of attorney with your attorney, you should take care to keep the original copy of your medical power of attorney and give copies of it to your patient advocates and medical providers. Give copies of your specific medical power of attorney to medical staff and any other person responsible for your medical file when you have surgery or medical procedures or any other time when you anticipate that you might be unable to speak or otherwise communicate your wishes regarding your health care. Discuss the terms of your specific durable medical power of attorney with your primary physician so that he or she is aware of your wishes and can be contacted if a situation should arise. If you travel frequently, you may want to take an extra step to ensure that your estate planning documents, including your medical power of attorney, are always with you. You may scan these documents and store them "in the cloud" so that you may access them anywhere you have Internet access. In addition, your scanned documents can be saved to a thumb drive and easily transported with you wherever you go. If you are traveling in another state and your medical power of attorney needs to be utilized while you are there, most states will honor the provisions of an out-of-state medical power of attorney that is properly drafted and executed.

IT IS NEVER TOO SOON

As I know from working with estate planning and motor vehicle accident clients, disability and death can happen to any of us at any time. That is why it's never too soon to create a medical power of attorney. In Michigan, anyone of sufficient legal capacity over the age of eighteen may create a medical power of attorney. For purposes of illustration of how it's never too soon to create your estate plan, I will relay the story of a young Floridian woman named Terri Schiavo. Her story made national headlines in the late 1990s. Ms. Schiavo, at age twenty-six, suffered a severe brain injury and as a result lived only in a persistent vegetative state. Her husband and her parents carried on an epic legal battle against each other that lasted from 1998 to 2005. At the heart of their dispute was whether to take away Ms. Schiavo's life support treatment, specifically a feeding tube, and allow her to die. Mr. Schiavo believed that his wife would never choose to live in a vegetative state. Ms. Schiavo's parents, however, believed that Terri Schiavo would choose life, in any capacity, over certain death (if the feeding tube and/or ventilator were removed).

The problem for the courts was, What did Terri Schiavo want? No one knew. Before her brain injury, she had never specifically discussed her life-care wishes with anyone with any degree of clarity. Ultimately, courts have ruled that for a party's intent regarding life and death decisions to be clear, such intent needs to be in writing and signed by the party. In Ms. Schiavo's case, eventually her feeding tube was removed and she was allowed to die in 2005. If Ms. Schiavo had a medical directive letting her loved ones know how she wanted to be medically cared for in that situation, her family may never have had to go through a seven-year-long legal battle.

This just goes to show that it is never too early to establish a medical directive. Many people in their twenties, like Ms. Schiavo, believe that they will have a long time before they need anything like a medical directive. Obviously, at Barberi Law we hope you live a long and healthy life, but a little early preparation could go a long way to saving yourself and your family a lot of agony in such a tragic event.

REVOCATION OF MEDICAL POWER OF ATTORNEY

You may choose to revoke your medical power of attorney at any time, in any manner, and by any means of communication. This means that you can revoke your medical power of attorney simply by speaking words to that effect as long as there are no issues regarding your competency. However, your revocation is not effective until others are aware of it. If you choose to revoke your medical power of attorney, it is best to give written notice to your patient advocates and anyone who has a copy of your medical power of attorney so that you can be sure that your new wishes are understood by all.

FINANCIAL POWER OF ATTORNEY

A financial power of attorney is a tool used by estate planners to give directions and authority to another person as to how you wish to have financial, business, and personal matters managed in the event that you are no longer able to do so. Even if you are able to manage your own affairs, a financial power of attorney is also used to have someone else assist you with such tasks.

Financial institutions, such as banks and credit unions, often have their own policies regarding how they process and honor financial powers of attorney. The following is a list of examples of how different banking institutions handle powers of attorney:

- Request that a copy of your power of attorney be placed on file with them.
- Request that an attorney-in-fact completes a form and mails it, along with a copy of your power of attorney, to them.

A power of attorney can be specific or general. An example of a specific power of attorney is when one individual gives another individual the power to act on his or her behalf to sell a particular parcel of property. As previously stated, I suggest making a person's financial power of attorney as all encompassing as possible so that the financial power of attorney can do almost anything the principal could do. There are a few things that Michigan law does not allow an attorney-in-fact to do, but other than those acts prohibited by law, an attorney-in-fact can do almost anything that the principal could do. For example, an attorney-in-fact can pay bills, deposit checks, sell and purchase real estate, hire professionals and borrow and lend money on an individual's behalf.

An "attorney-in-fact" is the individual, who may or may not be a lawyer, who is given written authority to act on another's behalf, especially by a power of attorney.

When your attorney-in-fact deals with a third party (e.g., utility company, credit union, etc.), the third party will want proof that your attorney-in-fact has the authority to act on your behalf. Your durable power of attorney will need to provide the third parties with that proof. So, before your attorney-in-fact can act on your behalf, copies of your durable power of attorney must be presented to third parties and an acceptance form must be signed. Remember that a copy of your durable power of attorney is as effective as your original durable power of attorney.

Your power of attorney operates during your lifetime, is effective during your incapacity, and terminates upon your death. You still have legal ownership of all your property while your power of attorney is in effect. Your attorney-in-fact has the power to make decisions based on your instructions included in your written durable power of attorney document and has a fiduciary duty to act in your best interest. You and/or ultimately your estate, as the case may be, will have legal remedies if your attorney-in-fact abuses these powers. Your attorney-in-fact is required to follow your orders and should not intimidate you into following his or her orders. Any self-dealing by the attorney-in-fact must be justified by the attorney-in-fact if called on by the court to answer questions about why your money or asset was used to benefit the attorney-in-fact.

EFFECTIVE UPON EXECUTION OR INCAPACITY

Some powers of attorney are written so as to only be effective upon incapacity, for example, when a court makes a determination that the giver of the power (the principal) is incapacitated or when two physicians declare that the giver of the power is unable to manage his or her financial affairs due to incapacity or disability. Most powers of attorney, however, are made to be effective immediately.

This means that your attorney-in-fact can start acting on your behalf the day that you sign your durable power of attorney. (This is different from your medical power of attorney, when your patient advocate may only make decisions and act on your behalf when two physicians or a physician and a licensed psychologist have declared that you are unable to participate in making your own medical decisions.) Your attorney-in-fact can continue to act on your behalf when you are incapacitated. I almost always draft my financial powers of attorney to be as general and all encompassing as possible and effective immediately. This makes the power of attorney much more valuable, and the principal's financial institutions, especially banks, will be able to rely on the power of attorney immediately without the need to determine whether they have been supplied with sufficient external evidence of a person's medical condition. Often, financial institutions will actually require a court order rather than just a doctor's signature as sufficient evidence of a person's mental or physical incapacity.

REVOCATION OF POWER OF ATTORNEY

As long as you are legally mentally competent, you may choose to revoke your power of attorney at any time, in any manner, and by any means of communication. If you choose to revoke your durable power of attorney, it is best to document your revocation and provide written notice to your attorneys-in-fact to that effect. Until they receive notice that you have revoked your durable power of attorney, they can still act on your behalf, which may result in them not meeting your wishes. You should also provide written notice about your revocation to financial institutions and other organizations that have a copy of your power of attorney on file.

It is also important to understand that after a person's death, any power of attorney previously executed by the decedent becomes "powerless" and is null and void. Once a person dies, the only individual authorized to act on behalf of the deceased individual is either a trustee of a trust created by the decedent while competent or a personal representative whose authority to act on behalf of the deceased has been authorized by a probate court order, pursuant to either a will submitted through probate or after being nominated and appointed by the probate court in the case of an intestate estate (when a person died without a will). There are cases in which trusts are actually created by operation of law after a party has died, but for purposes of this book, a discussion of this complicated situation is not undertaken.

POSSIBLE ABUSE

If not handled correctly, a financial power of attorney is a document that has the potential to be abused by others. These documents have been used by people to commit crimes by stealing money and other property. Sometimes, the wrong people are chosen to be attorneys-in-fact, and they take advantage of the situation and access to someone else's money, which is why it's important to carefully choose who you want to manage your finances if you are unable to do so yourself. Avoid appointing people who have a history of financial problems and/or addictions. You should try to appoint people who are responsible with money and are financially independent.

A *"personal representative"* is the person who marshalls and protects the assets of the estate, acts to distribute assets of the estate, and takes care of the estate's financial matters. Under previous law, this person was formerly referred to as the estate's executor or executrix.

WHEN THE COURT BECOMES INVOLVED: CONSERVATORSHIP AND GUARDIANSHIP

Sometimes your family or loved ones may feel that you are unfit to make medical or financial decisions on your own. If that situation arises, and if you have not previously executed a medical power of attorney and/or a durable financial power of attorney, a family member or interested party may have to involve a court to establish a conservatorship or a guardianship on your behalf. Many times the same person is appointed for both roles. It is almost always more expensive to have a conservator and guardian appointed than it is to take preventative action by creating an estate plan. It not only saves money but also relationships, which can deteriorate once a family becomes involved in a court case. In addition, a court case makes private matters public, such as an elderly parent's mental state or family squabbles.

CONSERVATORSHIP

A conservator is an individual appointed by the court to manage the estate and finances of another person in the event that the individual is no longer fit to perform the task. The conservator will be responsible for all of the financial obligations of the individual, such as resolving debt, paying expenses, and selling assets, as applicable. A conservatorship is monitored by the probate court to ensure that fair and responsible decisions are being made on behalf of the incapacitated party.

GUARDIANSHIP

If a medical directive isn't in place, a court-ordered guardianship will be required before anyone will be allowed to make medical decisions for a patient. There are many disadvantages to a guardianship:

- The court-appointed guardian may not be the person who the patient would have chosen to make important decisions.
- The guardian may be limited in the type of decisions he or she can make.
- It can strain family relationships.
- It is much more expensive than preparing a medical directive in advance of the principal's incapacity

The court-appointed guardian will be charged with ensuring the incapacitated person's health, well-being, maintenance, and day-to-day care (although the guardian need not actually have to personally provide such day-to-day care). A guardian is not required to be a relative of the person in need. The person a court appoints to be a guardian can be a friend, neighbor, or lawyer who has been determined to be fit to care for the person and to look out for the person's best interests. In most circumstances, a guardian will not be given authority by the probate court to execute a DNR order on behalf of the incapacitated individual.

CHAPTER 3

SPECIFIC GOALS WHEN PLANNING FOR DEATH

Estate planning attorneys help people plan for how to distribute their assets after death and how to ensure that their loved ones are cared for after their death by using wills, trusts, beneficiary designations, paid-on-death or transfer-on-death accounts, deeds, and other estate planning tools. A good first step in planning how you want your assets distributed and how you want your loved ones cared for after your death is to think about what specific goals you want to accomplish. Following is a list of commonly expressed goals that people may have when it comes to estate planning.

- I want to decide who will care for my minor children if I die or am unable to care for them myself.
- I want to leave enough to ensure that my parents are cared for after I die.
- I want my health and financial matters to be as private as possible, both before and after my death.
- I want to reduce any tax implications for myself and my loved ones.
- I don't want my family to have to go to court, and I want to minimize the expenses to my family.
- I don't want my children's spouse(s) or former spouse(s) to receive any of my children's or grandchildren's inheritance.
- I want to ensure that my loved ones who need or receive government benefits don't become disqualified from receiving them if I leave them an inheritance.
- I want to ensure that one or more of my family members does not receive an inheritance from me.
- I want to give directly to my grandchildren, instead of their parents.

- I want to make sure my business is transferred to the right people.
- I want to make sure my spouse has enough resources to be cared for properly for the rest of his or her life.
- I want to ensure my children receive a college education.
- I want to decide who will make medical decisions for me when I can't.
- I want to ensure that my child(ren)'s inheritance is protected from a stepparent.
- I want to take care of my spouse and my children from a previous marriage.
- I want to leave a charitable gift to one or more charities.
- I want to let my loved ones know my wishes regarding burial, funeral, cremation, and so on.

EXPANDING ON YOUR AFTER-DEATH ESTATE PLANNING GOALS

As the preceding "I want to" list reflected, there are many goals that people have when it comes to estate planning. Most people want to make sure their minor and adult children are taken care of, and some people want to leave a legacy for their family. Knowing what your goals are for estate planning can help your estate planning lawyer craft a plan to maximize your ability to meet those goals. Following, I will address five common goals that many people have when it comes to estate planning.

FIVE COMMON GOALS THAT PEOPLE HAVE WHEN IT COMES TO FORMULATING AN ESTATE PLAN

1. Providing for Your Family

It is human nature to want to make sure that your family is taken care of after your death. Proper estate planning ensures that your family will continue to be supported financially. When you are no longer around to take care of your family's needs, a plan must be put into place to make sure that the lifestyle that has been established can be maintained. In the absence of a solid plan, your family could be left without the financial support that they need to survive, at one of the most devastating times of their lives.

2. Naming a Guardian, Conservator, and/or Trustee for Minor Children

No parents want to have to think about who will care for their children if they die before the children turn eighteen. But it's important to set out your wishes for who you want to care for your children and who you want to manage their inheritance. If you don't make your wishes known, a probate court judge will decide whom your children will live with and who will be responsible for managing their inheritance without considering your wishes on those subjects. If you will be leaving a large inheritance to your children, any number of relatives with questionable motives may come out of the woodwork offering to care for your children.

One of the more common goals for estate planning is to shield your children from these harsh realities and ensure that they have a quality caretaker in your absence. It's important to nominate a guardian, conservator, and possibly a trustee for your children, and estate planning provides you with the opportunity to do so.

3. Choosing the "Right" Personal Representative

If you have a friend or family member whom you trust and you would like to make sure that he or she is the personal representative of your estate, then an estate plan takes on added importance. Your personal representative is given the authority to oversee all of the asset distributions following your death and is to adhere to your wishes. There are a wide range of duties that need to be taken care of after a person dies, so choosing a personal representative who is up to the task grants you peace of mind. Asset distribution is one of the most difficult things that has to be done following a person's death. Nominating a personal representative, and alternate personal representatives, in your estate planning documents allows you to place that responsibility in the hands of people you trust to carry out your wishes.

4. Designating Beneficiaries

There is no reason why a person should allow valuable property to fall into the wrong hands. However, when you don't take the time to name beneficiaries in a properly executed estate plan, this is precisely what can happen. Unless you have designated who is to receive your assets by estate planning, you have zero ability to make sure that your loved ones receive what you want them to receive, and you could be setting up your family for a long, drawn out battle in probate court.

When you don't name beneficiaries, your assets will be distributed according to the laws of the State of Michigan, as opposed to going to the people you have chosen. While choosing a personal representative who knows your wishes for distribution in advance of your death does help in these instances, the representative needs an estate plan to work with to ensure the correct distribution. During family squabbles over valuable or sentimental objects, it is best to have an estate plan in place so everyone knows your wishes.

5. Decreasing Your Loved Ones' Legal Fees and Taxes

When thinking about creating an estate plan, many people want to be certain that their loves ones are not burdened with unnecessary taxes, legal fees, other expenses related to their death, and their assets and debts. An estate planning attorney can help you create an estate plan that limits the potential financial burden that may be placed on your loved ones following your death. Just having a will that sets forth your nomination for a personal representative and who will receive which assets goes a long way to reducing the legal expenses, costs, and fees that your estate and/or loved ones may otherwise incur.

Planning your estate also significantly decreases the chances that your loved ones will be forced into a lengthy probate court proceeding. Estate planning can help significantly reduce legal fees and ensure that your loved ones do not spend months in court.

WHAT HAPPENS WITHOUT AN ESTATE PLAN?

If you haven't created an estate plan, the State of Michigan has created a plan for you called "intestate succession." Essentially, the state decides who will receive your property and who will be in charge of your assets.

For a married couple with children, if one of them dies today, leaving the other spouse alive, under the laws of intestacy, the first $221,000 (2015 amount, originally $150,000 in 2000, but indexed for inflation, and this amount changes each October) of the property goes to the surviving spouse and one-half of the balance is divided

equally 50/50 between the spouse and the children of the deceased. If there is no surviving spouse, then all children equally share the remainder of the assets. After the surviving spouse dies, that person's property would pass to the descendants, as the case may be.

In a case that I was involved in, a single gentleman owned a very modest house in downtown Mt. Pleasant, probably worth, at most, $60,000. When he executed his original will, while in his forties, he provided that upon his death, all of his real and personal property would go to his church. Some thirty years later, due to deaths in this single gentleman's family, he inherited a very large family farm that had been in his family for over 100 years. The value of this farm property ended up being several hundred thousand dollars. After reviewing the estate planning documents of other family members, it was clear to me that everyone "assumed" that eventually another family member would end up with the family farm, and through their estate planning, would keep the family farm "in the family." When I was contacted, no one knew about the existence of this thirty-year-old will that had been drafted for this single gentleman. After the single gentleman died, it was assumed that he had never executed a will and that he died intestate. After pleadings were properly filed with the Isabella County Probate Court to open an intestate estate and to have another family member appointed as the personal representative of the decedent, the existence of the thirty-year-old will (which had been filed with the Probate Court for safekeeping) came to light. The sad ending to this story for the family was that the family members were shocked to learn that the family farm, consisting of over 200 acres of prime farming real estate, now belonged to a church and not to any surviving family members of the decedent. There is no doubt in my mind that when this gentleman first executed his will, (drafted by another attorney), he likely would have chosen to leave the family farm to family members rather than the church. Sadly, because his will was drafted in this manner—"whatever real and personal property owned at his death ... went to the church"— that is the way the court interpreted his will. The church got everything, including the family farm, and his family members received nothing. Is that what he really wanted? We will never know, but I doubt it. Again, this is the reason estate plans, even if drafted by an attorney, need to be revisited every few years and updated or something that no one ever wanted to have happen may happen. Generally, assets that are subject to probate are those that are held in the deceased person's name alone. Therefore, jointly owned assets (real estate, bank accounts, etc.) are not subject to probate. Instead, the deceased person's interest in the asset automatically passes upon his or her death to the other owner(s). Other assets that are considered to pass automatically upon death include assets that are payable upon death (often bank/credit union accounts) and assets for which a beneficiary has been designated (401(k)'s, IRA's, life insurance, etc.).

Fortunately, you can create your own customized estate plan designed to meet your needs and goals and replace the State of Michigan's plan. An estate plan can also give your loved ones directions about what to do when you are incapacitated, in addition to what to do after your death. Do you wish to be cremated? If so, it's not a wise idea to put such wishes in your will. You can execute a separate document so that when your loved ones begin to probate your will they don't find out they had you buried when that was against your wishes. Accordingly, estate plans can help reduce family squabbles, expenses, and anxiety in times of great stress.

WILL OR TRUST?

Outside of transfer-on-death accounts, paid-on-death accounts, beneficiary designations, and jointly owned property, the methods by which to transfer assets after death include intestate succession (as discussed earlier), wills, and trusts. Most estate plans take one of two forms: will-based estate plans or trust-based estate plans. There is a lot of information floating around about whether you should use a will or a trust to transfer your assets upon your death. There is no one right answer for everyone. The tool that is best for you to use to transfer your assets depends on your family's situation and how comfortable you feel with managing your assets.

A will is a document that a person over the age of eighteen creates and signs which sets forth how that person wants his or her assets distributed after death and who will carry out those wishes. In addition, a person creating a will can also nominate a guardian and conservator for his or her children in the will. Some parents of minor children also create testamentary trusts as part of their wills from which a trust will be created only if certain circumstances exist. A trust, on the other hand, is an agreement that one or more persons (grantor[s], settlor[s], or trustmaker[s], hereinafter referred to as grantor[s]) create to manage and distribute certain assets. The grantor(s) nominate one or more persons or professionals (trustee[s]) to manage and distribute the trust assets. While the grantors are alive and well, most often, they are the initial trustees. A trust needs to be funded to be of any value, so after a trust agreement is signed, steps need to be taken to fund the trust. Examples of ways to fund a trust are general assignments of personal property, executed warranty or quitclaim deeds conveying real estate interests into a trust, executed lady bird deeds to transfer real estate into a trust upon death, beneficiary designations, and established bank accounts in the name of the trust's trustee(s). Trust assets generally pass outside of probate court, unless there is a dispute and a lawsuit is filed regarding the same. Trusts allow the creators to exercise more control over their assets, even many years after their deaths.

The person whom you nominate in your will to carry out your wishes is called your personal representative. It is commonly advised that, in addition to your first choice for a personal representative, you nominate one or more "backups" to act as personal representative(s) if your first choice is unavailable to act. A will is only effective after your death and until all of the property is distributed. A trust is effective both during your life and after death.

Wills are subject to probate, which means that to administer a will, a probate court file will need to be opened and a probate judge will oversee the distribution of your assets as set forth in your will. Some view the probate process in a negative light because there are court and attorney fees involved, and it is also puts forth your personal business in a public forum—a court record. On the other hand, passing on your assets to your beneficiaries via a will is often a very simple way to do so when compared to using a trust, which is more complicated to manage over time.

Another consideration is cost. Generally, a will is less expensive to create, but it may or may not result in increased court costs and fees when it comes to administer the terms of your will. A trust, in contrast, is generally more expensive to set up and also to maintain over time because it is necessary to ensure that your beneficiary designations on certain accounts and assets that you acquire over time are titled properly to be distributed pursuant to the terms of your trust.

THE POWER OF TIME

One advantage to utilizing a trust versus a will to distribute your assets is that it allows you to control the distribution of your assets long after your death. For example, let's take the situation of a young family with two minor children. The couple has a will which provides that their children will equally share their assets. The couple dies in a car accident, leaving their two young children. The couple's assets will be managed by a conservator who is appointed by a probate judge, and when each child reaches the age of eighteen, he or she will receive a share of the parents' assets. At eighteen, most people are not mature enough to manage the receipt of a large sum of money. A typical eighteen-year-old will spend a good portion of that money on a car, clothing, and disposable items that teenagers like. Many middle-aged adults have a hard time managing the receipt of a large sum of money, so giving an eighteen-year-old a large sum of money is a huge burden at that age. With a trust, parents can direct that a child's inheritance be spent in certain ways—for college education or the down payment on a home. In addition, with a trust, parents can direct that a child receive a certain portion of the inheritance at different events in the child's life. For example, the child can receive one-third at twenty-one, one-third at twenty-five, and one-third at thirty years old or a certain percentage upon graduation from college.

PROTECTING YOUR BENEFICIARIES FROM THEIR CREDITORS

In addition, trusts can have the benefit of protecting a beneficiary from creditors and ensuring that he or she continues to receive government benefits without being disqualified for the same. A properly drafted trust can provide that, instead of providing a beneficiary with a large sum of money, the beneficiary is given certain amounts according to needs, so that the beneficiary is not disqualified from the receipt of certain benefits, such as disability benefits. Further, if a beneficiary has a judgment against him or her and a creditor intends to collect the amount due out of the beneficiary's bank account, instead of providing that beneficiary with a sum of money that would then be subject to collection by the creditor, the trustee of the trust can pay expenses on behalf of the beneficiary, such as rent, mortgage, student loan, and so forth.

Trusts, generally, provide more flexibility to accommo-date the changing needs of family members over the years compared to the straightforward terms set out in most wills. However, they are more complicated to understand and utilize. If you crave simplicity, a will alone may be the best choice for you. If you want to cover a variety of situations that may arise and you don't mind a bit of work, a trust usually is the better option for you and your family.

> *Wills are more straightforward and simple than trusts but require court action to accomplish the decedent's wishes. However, trusts provide more flexibility to cover a variety of situations and no court action is normally required to carry out the decedent's wishes.*

THE USE OF BENEFICIARY DESIGNATIONS

I can't talk about asset distribution without touching on the use of beneficiary designations and paid-on-death or transfer-on-death accounts. Much of our assets today are held by a financial institution: 401(k)s, IRAs, bank accounts, life insurance, and so on. These assets pass automatically to the named beneficiaries upon the owner's death, and, generally, they don't require the involvement of a probate court to transfer. Often the holder of the asset will require a death certificate and proof of identity of the named beneficiaries and then the institutions will transfer the asset to the beneficiary. Most married people name their spouses as their primary beneficiary and their children as contingent beneficiaries to share in equal amounts. It is also possible to name the trustee of a trust as a beneficiary of an estate. Beneficiary designations are very useful tools to transfer assets to others upon death. However, often these designations can be forgotten or overlooked when people draft their estate planning documents. Not updating and coordinating these beneficiary designations with estate planning documents are big mistakes and can destroy overall plans set out in a will and/or trust.

LADY BIRD DEEDS

Similar to beneficiary designations, lady bird deeds (named after President Lyndon Johnson's wife) can be used to transfer real estate automatically to others upon a person's death. Generally, to transfer real estate after the owner's death, an order permitting a transfer will need to be obtained from a probate court, unless the owner owned the property jointly with another, the property was owned by a trustee of a trust, or the owner had executed a lady bird deed to transfer the property to someone else upon the owner's death or to a trustee of a trust. Currently, this is the preferred way to own real estate for many people because of its numerous benefits: it avoids probate, provides for a quick transfer upon death, avoids the application of estate recovery against the property, preserves the owners' rights to do what they wish with the property while alive, and prevents beneficiaries from attaching their debts to the property to the detriment of the owner.

WHY YOU STILL NEED A WILL (EVEN WITH A TRUST)

Even if you're going to have a trust, or more than one trust, as part of your estate plan, you still need a will. The will may be what is referred to as a "pour-over" will, which means that anything that you have not previously titled in the name of your trust will be "poured over" into one or more of your trusts. A pour-over will is designed to make sure that any assets you might own at the time of or as a result of your death find their way into one or more of the trusts that you have created as part of your estate plan.

As an example, if a person dies as a result of someone else's negligence, say for instance in an auto accident, the estate of the deceased can bring an action against a party responsible for causing the person's death and seek monetary damages for any conscious pain and suffering as a result of the accident that was experienced by the decedent prior to death. Additionally, any money recovered for the deceased person's pain and suffering becomes an asset of the estate and, obviously, such an asset could not have been placed into a person's trust prior to the motor vehicle accident. Additionally, sometimes people acquire ownership in a business venture or in real estate and forget to title their ownership interest into one or more of their trusts. By having a pour-over will, individuals make sure that "forgotten or unknown assets" still get placed into a trust to be distributed as part of their estate plan.

I can recall a couple meeting with me regarding their estate plan. I drafted two pour-over wills, powers of attorney, and a revocable living trust for them. Eight or nine years later, they sold their house in downtown Mt. Pleasant and bought a new house. When they executed their estate planning documents, I also advised them, in writing, that should they ever later acquire an interest in real estate that they needed to make sure they titled their new real estate in their name, as trustees, of their revocable living trust.

After the death of the last spouse to survive, one of their children, who had been designated as the alternative personal representative and successor trustee of her parents' trust, contacted me due to problems with selling the newly acquired real estate. Unfortunately, her parents' new house had been titled only in her parents' name, as individuals, and was not titled in the name of the couple, as trustees of their trust. As a result, we now had to admit the last surviving spouse's will into probate to pour-over the newly acquired real estate into their trust so that it could then be sold by the trustee. In the probate practice area, lawyers call this type of probating, probating "a standby will," which means you stand by and wait for the asset to be poured over into the trust so it can distributed according to the terms of the trust. In our case, this meant that the trustee had to stand by and wait for the will to be probated before the real estate could be sold. At a minimum, this required the trustee to wait 120 days after placing a notice in the local newspaper requesting any creditors to submit a claim before the personal representative could safely execute a personal representative deed transferring the real estate into the trust.

It's this type of a scenario that causes people to be frustrated because it causes them to have to wait a significant period of time before they can finalize their parents' estate. Had one of the parents revisited their estate planning documents and met with an attorney to make sure that any necessary updates in their estate plan were completed, then this waiting period could have been avoided, and it is likely that no probating of either of their wills would have been required. In this case, the review process would have discovered that the couple needed to retitle the newly acquired real estate such that the real estate would have been owned by the couple's trust. This would have avoided having to probate the pour-over will of the last surviving parent.

MANY DIFFERENT TYPES OF TRUSTS

There are many different types of trusts that can be utilized to accomplish an individual's estate plan goals. There can be trusts for grandchildren that might be much different than a trust set up to benefit children. Also trusts can be established to take advantage of assets owned during a person's lifetime and earmark such assets to go to a particular charity, as the beneficiary of such trust, at the time of the trust maker's death. Such trusts are known as charitable remainder trusts and utilizing the same can provide great tax benefits to the makers of such trusts while preserving the right to income from such assets during the trust maker's lifetime. There also are trusts that are set up solely to pay estate taxes (Irrevocable Life Insurance Trusts). Such trusts typically utilize life insurance proceeds to fund the payment of a person's estate taxes and to offset income taxes paid by a person's beneficiaries on distributions from qualified retirement accounts. This is why it's very important to consult with an elder law attorney and explore all of the options available to ensure that what you want to happen with your assets is best for you, your family, and your beneficiaries.

CHAPTER 4

MEDICAID PLANNING

The cost of nursing home care is ever increasing. Currently, nursing home care expenses start at approximately $8,000 per month. If you or your spouse need nursing home care for several months, or even years, and you have to pay the monthly expenses out of pocket, it could quickly wipe out your entire retirement savings and investment accounts. The federal Medicaid program that is administered by the State of Michigan pays nursing home care expenses for qualifying individuals. Qualification for Medicaid nursing home paid care is based on your income and assets, and individuals who meet the low income and asset requirements qualify for assistance from the program.

Although long-term care may be inevitable for us or our loved ones, it does not mean that we must spend all we have worked for and saved to pay for it. Understanding the rules applicable to qualifying for Medicaid benefits is critical to ensure that the money we have saved is not needlessly expended on the costs of nursing home care.

Although it can be tempting to try to apply for Medicaid benefits on your own, without assistance from a knowledgeable lawyer, a simple mistake or oversight could result in a denial, costing thousands of dollars. With so few law firms offering Medicaid qualification assistance in the central and mid-Michigan area, I and my estate planning and elder law legal team provide families in the surrounding area planning services for long-term nursing home care.

The idea of receiving government assistance, a government "handout," or "welfare," might seem repugnant to some people. However, I will ask you to think of Medicaid benefits in this way: If you have worked for thirty years or more, paid all of your taxes, and saved for your retirement, do you think it is fair for your entire savings to be used to pay for nursing home expenses, such that you or your spouse become impoverished? Or, that your children or grandchildren, who you hoped could use their inheritance to pay for college or a home, be denied that opportunity, when there is a government program available to help people in your situation? Have you ever felt that the government just continues to take more and more from its citizens? So, why would you turn down planning for this opportunity when the government says it's ready to help you pay for this expense?

PROTECTING YOUR ASSETS

It is possible to protect your life's savings, not leave your spouse impoverished, leave an inheritance to your children and grandchildren, *and* receive Medicaid benefits (payment for your nursing home care). Those goals do not have to be mutually exclusive.

If you do not currently meet Michigan's standards required to qualify for Medicaid benefits, it's best to meet with an attorney who regularly practices in this area of law. There are many attorneys whose estate planning and elder law practice consists of drafting wills, trusts, and powers of attorney but completely omits helping families qualify for Medicaid assistance. Many lawyers avoid this area of law because the regulations frequently change and the various planning techniques that need to be employed are very complex.

Lawyers whose elder law practice includes Medicaid planning must stay up to date on Medicaid regulations, as they typically change every ninety days. For example, in August 2014, the Department of Human Services (DHS) changed its position regarding trusts, commonly known as Solely for the Benefit Of trusts or SBO trusts. For many years prior, the DHS permitted the use of SBO trusts in Medicaid planning. An SBO trust is an irrevocable trust solely for the benefit of the community spouse. Typically, one of the adult children would serve as trustee. The trustee then manages the assets in the trust and every year transfers a portion of the principal of the trust to the community spouse (the spouse who does not reside in a nursing home), who is the sole lifetime beneficiary. These trusts were commonly used tools in Medicaid planning and were often the go-to resource to obtain qualification for Medicaid benefits for married couples in which one spouse lived in a nursing home and the other remained in the community. Now that their use is no longer permitted, Medicaid planning attorneys were left to come up with creative alternate planning tools to help clients qualify for Medicaid benefits. This is why it is more important than ever to seek assistance from an elder law attorney who continuously monitors changes in DHS's rules and regulations and develops new methods for helping clients who are seeking Medicaid benefits.

In addition, currently the value of one's vehicle is not counted toward the assets looked at to determine

Medicaid eligibility. So, you could own a Lamborghini or a BMW and still qualify for Medicaid if your other "countable assets" total less than the maximum allowable amount. As a result of this regulation, many people who are looking to become qualified for Medicaid might consider purchasing a more expensive vehicle for their mother or father. This would convert a countable asset (cash) into a noncountable asset (a spouse's vehicle).

The expense required to pay an attorney to help persons qualify for Medicaid benefits, in most situations, will be wholly recouped in one to three months of otherwise paying for nursing home care. For example, if an attorney's fee for helping a married spouse qualify for Medicaid is $12,000 and that person's nursing home care expenses are $8,000 per month, the family will recoup the lawyer's fee in less than two months. So, for one year of nursing home care, your family's expense will be approximately $96,000 (paying out of pocket) or $12,000 (once qualified for Medicaid). Most nursing home stays average around three years, costing the family to liquidate approximately $300,000 of the family's hard earned assets. Doing this math, it's easy to see why it makes sense to quickly hire a competent elder law attorney to help qualify a person for Medicaid.

There are many hoops to go through when attempting to comply with Medicaid's planning rules and regulations.

Contacting and working with an experienced Medicaid planning attorney will help you qualify a person for Medicaid to pay for nursing home care quickly. An attorney experienced in Medicaid planning can counsel you on how to properly transfer assets and explain to you which assets count toward a person's total maximum and which do not. Once a person is approved to receive Medicaid benefits, they must obtain re-approval each year.

While many people are too proud and think they don't want any government handouts, Medicaid funding can be incredibly important to you and your family in times of great hardship. That being said, when I conduct estate planning seminars and workshops, I usually ask attendees, "After working thirty years, how many of you want to see your life's savings be paid out within three years or less because you have to enter a nursing home?" The response: "Let the record reflect, no hands appear." I rest my case.

MICHIGAN'S ESTATE RECOVERY

You may have heard the term "estate recovery" in regard to Medicaid, or you may have heard something along the lines of "the State will take your house" if you receive Medicaid benefits. The State of Michigan has implemented estate recovery; it was the last state in the country to do so. It is the state's attempt to recoup the money it paid on the behalf of Medicaid benefit recipients, a large portion of which is for nursing home care. Estate recovery only applies to people who received Medicaid benefits, are over the age of fifty-five, and began receiving benefits after 2007.

"Estate recovery" is the procedure whereby the State of Michigan attempts to recover the value of benefits conferred on a Medicaid beneficiary during such beneficiary's lifetime from assets passing through such beneficiary's probate estate.

After the death of a person who received Medicaid benefits, the Department of Health and Human Services will send a questionnaire to the person's personal representative or a family member asking him or her to fill out the same and return it. The department will review the questionnaire to determine whether there are any assets to be probated, and if so, it may move forward with filing a claim against the person's estate. Estate recovery only applies to probatable assets. So, those assets that pass automatically upon a person's death via a beneficiary designation or because the account was structured as a paid-on-death or a transfer-on-death account (bank accounts) are not subject to estate recovery by the State of Michigan. Likewise, real estate transferred pursuant to

Michigan Land Title Standard 9.3, commonly referred to as a lady bird deed, is also not subject to estate recovery. There are certain situations when the state will defer or choose not to file a claim against a person's estate, such as when the deceased left a surviving spouse or when an undue hardship is shown. Oftentimes, after someone's death, it is difficult to ascertain how assets were owned and the value of each. It's wise to seek the advice and counsel of an experienced elder law attorney to determine whether filing such a questionnaire is ever required or to review and help you complete the questionnaire to avoid costly mistakes.

MYTHS

There are numerous myths about Medicaid, which are caused because its rules are very peculiar and ever changing. There is a lot of misinformation about Medicaid and there is no shortage of "hot tips" about Medicaid. For example, one such hot tip is that you can give away $14,000 to each of your kids and that is okay when spending down to qualify for Medicaid assistance. In reality, it may prevent you from needing to file a gift tax return, but these gifts create a penalty period if you apply for Medicaid within sixty months of making such a gift. Some other myths include the state will take your home, you will have to give your assets away to protect them, and, if you give your assets away, you have to wait sixty months to qualify for Medicaid benefits. None of these myths are necessarily true. While you are alive, the state doesn't want your house. After you're death, the state would sell your house if there was any equity to be realized from such a sale to help recover the cost of your Medicaid assistance received during your lifetime subject to certain exceptions.   You can remain in control and still keep your assets, including your home, especially if you have a community spouse. You can qualify in short order with proper guidance, and even in a crisis situation, you can save a significant portion of your assets and, with proper planning, protect your home from any claims by the state after your death.

NUTS AND BOLTS OF MEDICAID

Medicaid eligibility is based on income and asset requirements. Currently, in 2015, there is no income limit for the community spouse, and the applicant's income must be less than the cost of care, often at the nursing home. For asset limits, the community spouse may have a minimum community resource allowance of $23,844 to a maximum of $119,220. The applicant must own less than $2,000 in countable assets. Plus, there are certain exemptions and exclusions.   There are two tests to determine eligibility: income and assets. For married applicants, the community spouse may retain one-half of the countable marital assets, not less than $23,844 or not to exceed $119,220 (2015), as well as a homestead (less than $543,000 in equity), one vehicle, and personal effects, among other exclusions.

Assets excluded (noncountable) for purposes of Medicaid eligibility include the following:

- Homestead (maximum $543,000 equity)
- Vehicle (broadly defined); the "Medicaid Cadillac"
- Term life insurance (and whole life insurance policies with a combined death benefit of less than $1,500)
- Personal effects
- Prepaid funeral contract (applicant only, $12,240)
- Burial space for qualified family members
- Burial space items for allowable family members (which can include casket, vault, and burial plot)
- Burial fund

Attorneys who are seasoned in Medicaid planning utilize different approaches to help clients qualify for Medicaid benefits. These methods include applying to a probate court for relief to improve a community spouse's income or increase a community spouse asset allowance and allow for a divestment trust to be established; entering into promissory notes with family members; purchasing a new motor vehicle; painting or renovating the home; creating immediate annuities; engaging in preplanning divestment trusts; and exploring long-term care insurance options.

THE LOOK BACK PERIOD

You may have heard of a five-year "look back period" regarding Medicaid or that you can't transfer any assets for five years prior to entering a nursing home or you won't qualify for Medicaid benefits. In actuality, there is a penalty period for transferring assets without receiving adequate consideration during the sixty months prior to applying for Medicaid benefits. That being said, our elder law legal team can help you determine the length of any penalty period applicable to your loved one. Generally, to calculate the penalty period, you divide the amount of the divestment by $8,084 (amount in 2015) and that will produce the term of the penalty period. For example, say you gave your son $50,000 as a gift two years ago and now you need nursing home care. Although eligible for Medicaid benefits, you will be subject to a private pay penalty for just over six months before the receipt of Medicaid benefits begins. To determine whether you have made any such transfers, DHS may want to look at your financial records to verify that a penalty period doesn't apply to you. It's important to be truthful and forthcoming when responding to DHS inquiries because all information provided to DHS, and answers given, subject you to the penalty of perjury should you misrepresent the facts.

CHAPTER 5

TOP SIX MISTAKES PEOPLE MAKE IN ESTATE PLANNING

1. TAKING THE DIY APPROACH TO ESTATE PLANNING

I understand people taking a do-it-yourself approach to many things in life: gardening, painting rooms in your house, even building a deck. Sometimes, it makes sense to do things yourself rather than to hire an expert to do them for you, especially when it can save you money. Most people can handle simple home repairs and maintenance, and the result will be nearly as good as if an expert performed the task. And with minor tasks and jobs, if the result is not what you wanted, the consequence is not severe. You can repaint the wall, have a friend or family member help you install the cabinet, or, if it becomes necessary, even break down and hire a professional to help you.

However, some things are best left to the professionals. For example, let's say you are preparing dinner and you accidentally cut your hand with a knife. Your hand starts bleeding heavily and the cut looks pretty deep. You can approach this situation in two different ways. The first is to treat the cut yourself. You can apply pressure to the wound, stitch it up yourself, and splash a little hydrogen peroxide on it, and chances are you will stop the bleeding. While you could temporarily take care of the problem, you might be causing more problems for yourself down the road. Your cut could become infected, likely won't heal properly, and could leave you with a nasty scar. You might even have to be hospitalized for the infection and undergo surgery to fix your botched stitch job.

Your other option is to immediately go to an emergency room and seek medical treatment from professionals— emergency medical providers, nurses, and doctors. These professionals will clean out your wound so that it's free from infection. A surgeon will look at the wrinkle lines in your hand and stitch your wound so that any remaining scar is almost undetectable. They will also treat any pain you have with prescribed medications. They will make sure you are healthy and taken care of before they send you on your way. You will probably have a follow-up appointment so that the surgeon can make sure your hand is healing as it should and that no problems have arisen since your surgery.

This example shows the difference between taking care of your estate plan on your own and having a professional take care of it for you. An estate planning attorney will make sure you don't run into legal problems down the road.

There are companies out there who purport to help you write your estate planning documents for you and for what they market as a reasonable price. If you take this approach, you may always wonder if your estate planning documents generated by a software program really meet all your needs. When you seek the advice of an experienced estate planning attorney, you are not paying for software-generated forms. You are paying for that person's education, experience, and advice that is specific to you and your loved ones.

If you find a form online for a quitclaim deed or a will, you don't know where that form originated. It could have been drafted according to California law or Florida law, which is very different from Michigan law. Each state has its own statutes and laws governing wills, powers of attorney, patient advocate designations, trusts, and so forth. If you draft a will on a form written for Tennessee law, your wishes may not be carried out in Michigan.

Using a will template or paying for a will generated by a company online are examples of how DIY estate planning can go wrong. Let's say you use this template or software to generate a will in which you leave everything to your father and to your minor children if your wife doesn't survive you. You think you're all set. But your life insurance policy is set so that you leave 100 percent of your policy to your father who you named as beneficiary before you were married. Now what happens? Your primary asset, your life insurance policy, will be automatically transferred to your father (pass outside of your will), and your wife and children are left with almost nothing. And, to top it off, your father will be under no legal obligation to share any portion of the life insurance proceeds with your wife or children, and they almost certainly will have no legal remedy to obtain any portion of the life insurance proceeds. But, you say, my father will do the right thing, won't he? That's called planning for destiny. What if your father has Alzheimer's disease or is otherwise incapacitated? No guardian or conservator could turn down this money to care for your father without legal issues being created.

The most important aspect of estate planning is how your assets are titled, and that is something that a form generated from software can't do for you. You can leave everything to your wife in your will, but life insurance has nothing to do with your will. In addition, LegalZoom won't tell you how to incentivize your children or grandchildren to get a good education by including certain provisions in your will or trust. Many parents don't want to pass on a lot of wealth at one time to children because they don't want to inhibit their children's drive to get jobs and support themselves. Instead, most parents want their wealth to be used as a safety net or utilized for education, to purchase a home, or to fund a business. Most parents earned their assets the old-fashioned way, and they want to instill work ethic in their children. Online or preprinted forms don't tell you how to do that, but an estate planning attorney can.

This is why this book has been written. Often, in one situation, "what works" is a mistake in another situation. Estate planning is not nearly as expensive as you might think. Depending on the complexity of your case, it's often better to spend $750 to $2,500 rather than using a one-size fits all approach that ends up not working. The more complex your estate planning issues, the more risk you have for error and the more planning is required. Accordingly, the complexity of your estate planning issues ultimately determines your legal expenses. Most importantly, you want to make sure that what you want to have happen actually does happen.

Even if you are a college professor, and I would be the first to admit that there are many college professors smarter than myself and other lawyers, it still makes sense to have a specialist advise you when you are doing your estate planning. You can afford it. As Abe Lincoln stated: "When you have yourself for a client, you have a fool for a client." Go get proper legal advice.

Accountants and financial planners may say they do estate planning, but only lawyers can do estate planning—draft the documents that will transfer assets and advise clients about the proper course of action. Accountants and financial planners can give you accounting and financial advice, but not legal advice. If something is challenged in court, only lawyers can go to court and make sure your wishes are followed.

Owning Property Jointly

A common estate planning strategy, again another DIY approach, is to add a child to a deed and to add a child on a financial account, giving that child instructions that once the parent dies, the child is to divide the property or the money in the bank account equally among the parent's other children. The parents cleverly think they have avoided probate and the necessity of having a will. Estate planning in this way is commonly referred to as the "poor man's will." The parents who add a child's name to a deed or to an account opens the parent up to a litany of potential problems.

The first problem is that when you own property jointly, you are exposing your jointly held asset to your co-owner's creditors, including a spouse, should the couple divorce. The co-owner can obtain financing and place a lien on your asset. If he or she doesn't follow through on his or her promise to pay back money borrowed, the creditor can seek repayment of the monies borrowed by taking back the security for the loan—your property.

Secondly, the co-owner may not follow your wishes. In Michigan, one joint tenant's ownership interest of real property that is owned by joint tenants with full rights of survivorship automatically passes to the other joint owner(s) upon death. The surviving joint owner has no legal obligation to follow your wishes to sell the property and equally divide the proceeds among the other children. The surviving owner could legally retain 100 percent ownership of the property. The other children would have no legal recourse to claim their share of your inheritance. The same goes for bank and credit union accounts. Most joint bank and credit union accounts are managed such that each owner can do what he or she wishes with the monies in the account. If you added one of your children to your bank account, while you are alive, your child will have the ability to draw down your account to zero, and it will be a struggle to have any legal recourse against that child. And, after your death, the monies in your jointly held bank account are automatically owned (100%) by the other joint owner, and he or she has no legal obligation to share the inheritance with anyone else.

Classic Case of the Failure of a DIY Estate Plan

I was retained by a Texas client whose father had called his son (my client) in May to inform him that he had attained his lifetime financial goal of amassing more than $1 million in cash. He just wanted his son to know this and to know that he had "taken care of everything" himself in terms of his estate planning and that when he died his son and two daughters (one who lived in Michigan) would each receive one-third of his estate. In July, sadly, the father called again, this time to advise his son that he had just been diagnosed with pancreatic cancer and was dying.   In the fall, after my client's father died, my client's half-sister sent her brother and sister checks for more than $100,000 each, advising them that "their father wanted them to have this money as their share of their father's estate." Because one-third of a million dollars didn't equate to $100,000, my Texas client contacted me and retained my firm, on a contingency basis, to pursue a full accounting of his father's estate.

After litigation was commenced, it was learned, among other things, that my client's father had put my client's half-sister's name on more than $1.4 million of certificates of deposit (CDs) at a local credit union. My client's father's DIY will had also divided his home equally to all three of his children. Unfortunately, my client's father had previously executed a deed in which he conveyed his house to himself and his Michigan daughter "as joint tenants with full rights of survivorship." The unintended consequences of such titling was to eliminate his home as an asset of his estate to be equally divided among his three children. As a result, equally dividing the value of my client's father's home did not occur, and the Michigan daughter took their father's home free from any claim of her half-siblings and the estate.

As the litigation continued, ultimately my client's position prevailed and resulted in a finding that when the father added the Michigan daughter's name on the CDs, such was done for purposes of convenience rather than to transfer ownership to the daughter upon his death. Clearly, my client's father's intent was "to avoid probate" by having the Michigan daughter cash in his CDs and distribute two-thirds of the proceeds, equally, to each of her two half-siblings. In finalizing the litigation, my Texas client and his sister each received a gross settlement in excess of $300,000. That being said, litigation expenses ate up some of the estate's proceeds that my client's father would have liked his children to have received as we convinced the court and the Michigan daughter of what her father intended to have been done with his CDs after his death. Had the father just consulted with an elder law attorney, for a nominal cost, what the father wanted to have happen would have happened without the siblings ending up in litigation and spending thousands of dollars in unnecessary legal fees.

Additionally, by titling property with yourself and one child, you leave yourself without a backup plan. If your co-owner predeceases you or becomes brain injured in a car accident or you both die simultaneously, there is no backup plan for your assets. With a brain injury, you may have to go to court to have a conservator appointed for your child, who is now incapacitated. If it is determined that your co-owner died after you, then the property you owned jointly will pass to his or her beneficiaries and/or heirs according to the co-owner's estate plan, trust, or the laws of intestacy if he or she did not have an estate plan. Your surviving children would have no legal recourse to claim their share of your inheritance. Rather, your jointly held property would pass to your co-owner's heirs and beneficiaries.

DIY Estate Plans Often Create Tax Issues

For persons with a large federal taxable estate, joint ownership with someone who is not your spouse can create a double taxation problem. The entire taxable amount will be subject to the federal estate tax, unless the surviving co-owner can show his contribution to the jointly held taxable asset. Then, upon the co-owner's death, the amount of the asset that is not consumed will be taxed a second time. Currently, Michigan does not have an estate tax, but there is a federal estate tax. The majority of estates will not be subject to the federal estate tax, which taxes estates with assets that value $5,450,000 in 2016 or higher at the rate of 40 percent. In addition, when you do sell the asset, your tax basis may end up being much lower than what it would have been had you received the asset through probate (with a step-up in your tax basis). In this situation you could pay thousands of dollars in capital gains taxes that could have been avoided by using a will or trust to transfer such assets to your beneficiaries upon your death. Joint ownership and transferring assets upon death via beneficiary designations can be excellent methods of transferring assets to loved ones, but it should be done with the advice of your estate planning attorney and in conjunction with your overall estate plan.

If you have created an estate plan by having a will and/or a trust, you may unwittingly undo all that planning by owning property jointly with someone else. As stated earlier, upon your death, jointly owned property transfers automatically and is owned by the co-owner. This means that the asset (bank account, real estate) passes outside of your will or trust. If that asset made up the majority of your estate, the provisions of your will to leave all of your assets equally to your three children may be for naught because now only one child may own 100 percent of one of your most valuable assets. The DIY approach is often planning for destiny—at Barberi Law we plan for certainty.

> *Top mistakes made when making an estate plan include taking the DIY approach; not taking care of life insurance; choosing the wrong estate planner; waiting until it's too late; not updating wills or estate plans; and not maximizing Social Security benefits.*

2. NOT TAKING CARE OF LIFE INSURANCE ISSUES

Simply having life insurance doesn't guarantee that your loved ones will be taken care of in the event of your death. It is crucial that you pay attention to the details of your insurance policy, carefully selecting a beneficiary and determining how the policy will be paid out. If you neglect to coordinate your life insurance policy with your overall estate plan, it can cause unexpected complications in the future.

Not Having Enough Life Insurance

When deciding on a life insurance policy, determining how much coverage you need can be a difficult decision.

If your goal is to make sure that your family can take care of your final expenses and still live comfortably after you are gone, then there are a lot of things to consider. In some cases, particularly when the decedent is the primary bread winner of the household, issues can arise for those left behind if the insurance payout is insufficient. A life insurance salesperson can help you calculate an amount of life insurance to purchase that will take care of your family's needs once you are gone. A general rule of thumb is that one should secure enough life insurance, at a minimum, to pay for funeral expenses, pay off any mortgages and any other jointly held debts (or individually held debts that are secured by property, which you wish to pass on to a loved one), and provide your family with enough money for living expenses for at least six months.

Leaving Benefits to a Child When They Are Too Young

Oftentimes, when selecting a beneficiary for your life insurance policy, your child or children are often your first choice, if you are not married, and your contingent, or co-first choice after your spouse, if you are married. If you name your child as a beneficiary outright before your child is ready to take on the responsibility of receiving such a large payout, many problems can arise. If you name your minor child as a beneficiary on a life insurance policy and you pass away before your child is eighteen years old, the life insurance proceeds you left your child will need to be managed by a conservator appointed by a probate court. However, upon your child reaching age eighteen, your child will be entitled to receive the remainder of the life insurance proceeds. And, as stated before, it's generally not a good idea to give an eighteen-year-old thousands and thousands of dollars. A better way to transfer life insurance proceeds to a child is to establish a trust to take your life insurance proceeds, which will then manage and payout such funds according to your wishes and time line. You can establish and fund a trust now or set up a testamentary trust through your will, which will only come into existence under certain circumstances.

Your Beneficiary Can Be Disqualified from Government Benefits

If your life insurance beneficiary is entitled to government benefits, you have to be careful when designating how that beneficiary will receive the inheritance or he or she may be at risk of losing governmental benefits. If your beneficiary is disabled, on Medicaid, or receives Social Security benefits based on financial need, for example, your beneficiary's benefits should be allocated to a trust rather than to the beneficiary directly. In that way, your beneficiary can still receive the government benefits he or she needs as well as the benefits from your life insurance proceeds to pay for expenses that the beneficiary's government benefits do not cover.

3. CHOOSING THE WRONG ESTATE PLANNER

Finding the right estate planner can be critical if you want your estate to be distributed efficiently and according to your wishes. You want to not only choose an attorney but also make sure that the estate planner has experience in estate planning and extensive knowledge of elder law. Hiring a professional can alleviate any worry you may have about mistakes being made or things being overlooked that may come back to haunt your family in the future. You should not rely on any forms provided to you by someone who is trying to sell you a financial product or service as proper estate-planning documents. It's also not wise to hire your brother-in-law who practices bankruptcy law to draft a "simple will" for you. Like you wouldn't ask your grandchildren's pediatrician to treat your artery blockage, you shouldn't seek estate-planning assistance from an attorney who does not regularly practice estate planning. Laws change frequently and the ways in which laws are interpreted by probate courts are ever changing. It's essential to keep up with these changes to provide proper legal advice on estate planning matters. As lawyers, we learn about a variety of areas of law in law school and when we are preparing for the bar exam, but after that, most attorneys focus on one, two, or three areas of law in which to practice, to the exclusion of the rest. So, although attorneys might have a vague recollection of what they learned about wills and trusts in law school, if they don't regularly practice estate planning, they are not well-equipped to draft your estate planning documents and advise you on beneficiary designations, jointly owned property, and funding your trust(s).

4. WAITING UNTIL IT'S TOO LATE

Most people are aware that it is in their best interest to plan for their future, but oftentimes they don't want to face the finality or stress of losing a loved one or passing away themselves. This fear and anxiety sometimes results in waiting to create an estate plan until it is too late. The phrase "better safe than sorry" certainly applies here. There are things in life that occur outside of your control, and it is best to make the hard decisions now before you lose the chance. In the event of an incapacitating injury, disability, or sudden death, determining how situations should be handled or how to pass on your assets can become that much more difficult if your wishes are unknown. Failure to plan your estate can lead to conflict among your family, delay in distributing your assets, difficulty receiving care, and other unexpected obstacles. Even though it may be difficult to think about possible sickness in your late years or the idea of leaving your family behind, they will be thankful that you planned ahead when the inevitable time comes.

You must have the legal capacity necessary to properly execute a valid patient advocate designation, durable power of attorney, will, trust, or deed; to enter into contracts; and to take other legal actions. If you wait too long to execute your power of attorney and become incapacitated, you can't execute one. When that happens, it ties the hands of people and organizations, and often, many things can't be done. Someone, usually a family member or friend, must petition the local probate court and ask to be appointed as your conservator and/or guardian. Conservators and guardians are limited in the actions they can take. Before they can take some actions, they must first obtain the probate court's approval. And guardians cannot sign a DNR order or otherwise authorize the removal of life support measures unless there is evidence of your intent and wishes that such should be done.

If you die without a will, the property that you own in your name alone will pass to your heirs according to the laws of intestacy in Michigan, which may not be how you wish your property to pass and be distributed. If you have minor children, it's possible that they will inherit their share of your estate when they turn eighteen. As stated, oftentimes, children are not mature enough to manage large amounts of money at only age eighteen. If you want your children's inheritance to pay for college or a down payment for their first homes, you need to establish your estate plan to make sure that happens. Otherwise, if you die intestate, without a will, your children may receive $100,000 when they turn eighteen and buy cars, clothes, televisions, games, phones, and everything rather than pay for college or save it for their first home.

5. NOT UPDATING YOUR WILL OR ESTATE PLAN

An estate plan is no good unless it is accurate and complete. One of the most common things that people overlook is updating their will or estate plan after it is initially drafted. Once you spend the time and effort to plan for your later years and decide what will happen to your assets, who gets what when you're gone, how your care will be handled, and the details involved in estate planning, many people file their documents away and forget them. This can be a big mistake because, let's face it, life happens. Relationships sometimes end and new ones begin, a beneficiary may pass on, or you may acquire additional assets and get rid of others. You can never plan for everything so it is a good rule of thumb to revisit your estate plan at least every three years.

6. NOT MAXIMIZING YOUR SOCIAL SECURITY BENEFITS

One of the worst mistakes you could make when it comes to estate planning is taking your Social Security retirement benefits at the wrong time. I know what you may be thinking: What do my Social Security retirement benefits have to do with planning my estate? Well, for most of us, our Social Security retirement benefits make up a good portion of our incomes during our last one, two, three, or four decades on this earth. If you want to help provide financially for your children or grandchildren or be in a position to give money charitably, Social Security retirement benefits are a great resource for doing so. And, if you take your benefits at the right time, you can maximize them and produce more income for yourself. Doing so allows you to live a fuller, richer, and better life—traveling, paying for quality medical and personal care, giving help to children and grandchildren, and so on—while you're here. It also gives you the ability to have more available assets to pass on to your loved ones after your death.   So what do I mean when I talk about the right time to receive Social Security retirement benefits? This right time is explained in the book *Get What's Yours – The Secrets to Maxing Out Your Social Security* by Laurence J. Kotlikoff, Philip Moeller, and Paul Solman. While visiting my cousins in New Hampshire, I came across this book at a bookstore and was intrigued by its premise. For many of us, it's a forgone conclusion about when we will start taking our Social Security retirement benefits. It's something we think about and then come to a decision on fairly quickly.

- I'll take it as soon as I can because
    — I need all the income I can get;
    — who knows how long I'll live; and
    — Social Security retirement benefits are my only retirement option.

- I'll take it when my spouse does.
- I'll take it when my spouse retires.
- I'll wait until I'm at my full retirement age so I can receive the full amount possible per month.

When it comes to financial planning, Social Security retirement benefits often receive short shrift despite the huge part they make up in our retirement income. Likewise, many people don't give Social Security retirement benefits much thought when it comes to thinking about their estate or their total assets. But if you think about it, for many years, Social Security retirement benefits have been the most reliable and consistent retirement investment most Americans have. Social Security retirement benefits are guaranteed by the U.S. government and are protected against inflation. Every January (almost), Social Security retirement benefits recipients' annual payment amounts are raised by the previous year's inflation rate. That being said, no increase occurred in 2016 due to no increase in the consumer price index (CPI) for 2015.

By way of an example to show how great a resource Social Security retirement benefits can be, consider this: A married couple who earned the payroll tax ceiling their entire lives has an asset in the form of Social Security retirement benefits in the approximate amount of $1.2 million if they take their benefits starting at age sixty-two. How many of us have that amount saved for retirement? And imagine how much greater that asset could be if that couple could wait longer than age sixty-two to begin taking their benefits. So, Social Security retirement benefits are no trivial investment and the timing of when one starts receiving those benefits should be carefully considered, as described later. As the authors of *Get What's Yours* write, "Figuring out what to apply for and when to do it is not simple. Indeed, Social Security is the most complicated 'simple' program you're ever likely to encounter."

In *Get What's Yours*, the authors sets forth the most important rule to follow when it comes to Social Security benefits:

Be Patient!

Take Social Security's best deal by waiting to collect for as long as possible—taking much higher benefits over somewhat fewer years.

As you may be aware, each year you wait to take your Social Security retirement benefits, you receive 8 percent more than you could have the year before (and that is before the annual inflation adjustment). Life expectancies are growing higher and higher for both men and women in the United States. Many people fear that they will die young and miss out on their Social Security retirement benefits, so they take them as soon as possible. But, the reality is that the majority of us live well into our eighties and beyond. We need to plan for that possibility as well as the possibility of death at an earlier age. If we live to ninety-five, can we afford it? That's where that extra 8 percent every year can really help give you a more comfortable life in your advanced elder years. With people living longer and longer, most of us should be concerned with outliving our retirement savings. And when it comes to taking care of your spouse, taking lesser benefits earlier also decreases the amount your spouse will receive as widow or widower benefits.

Your Social Security retirement benefits are reduced if taken early—before your full retirement age—and they increase greatly if you take them after your full retirement age. According to the authors of *Get What's Yours*, here are "[t]he raw numbers:

- Retirement benefits starting at 70 are 76 percent higher than those starting at 62.
- Spousal benefits are 43 percent higher at Full Retirement Age than at 62.
- Survivor benefits are 40 percent higher at Full Retirement Age than at 60."

The benefit of waiting to take your Social Security retirement benefits end when you turn seventy. Your benefits will never be any higher than they are when you are seventy so you shouldn't wait to take them past that age.

Generally it is best to wait as long as possible before starting to take your social security benefits.

CHAPTER 6

PROBATE AND ADMINISTRATION ESTATE

Following a person's death, the deceased's estate (that property which was owned in the individual's name alone) must be handled and distributed among the deceased's living heirs or beneficiaries according to the will. If the decedent has no will, then the estate will be distributed according to the laws of intestacy in Michigan. The distribution of property (that which is owned solely in that person's name and is not transferred by way of a beneficiary designation or joint ownership) after a person's death is known as "probating" an estate and is conducted in a probate court. Because the majority of estate cases can quickly get complicated, it's highly recommended that an attorney is consulted and retained to handle the probate proceedings. Attorneys who regularly practice estate planning and probate law are the best choices to handle probate cases. When probating a person's estate, there is a priority in which the person's estate must be used to pay debts, creditors, fees, and then beneficiaries. A commonly asked question of estate planning attorneys is whether a person's heirs will be responsible for payment of that person's debts after death. The answer is no, as long as the debt is in the deceased person's name alone. Some assets, such as homes, are encumbered by debts, like promissory notes secured by mortgages, and those pass subject to the debt owed. Once a probate court file is opened, notice must be given to known and unknown creditors of the probate proceedings and creditors are allowed to make a claim on the estate.

To give you a better idea of how probate proceedings are carried out in Michigan, I will give you a brief overview of how a will is probated in Michigan. In 2015, small estates (less than $22,000) can be probated in a relatively simple manner by using a petition and assignment, along with payment of a filing fee (currently only $25) and an inventory fee. Inventory fees are based on the dollar value of an estate. If the court accepts the petition, it will then proceed to dividing and distributing the estate.

For the handling of estates that are valued over $22,000, there are generally two options. You can choose to open a probate case either formally or informally. Informal proceedings take place once an application for the informal probate and/or for the appointment of a personal representative has been filed along with payment of the filing fee. If the court admits the will, a "register's statement" will be issued and a personal representative will be appointed by the court. A personal representative is the person who distributes the estate and takes care of the estate's financial matters. The personal representative is usually that person who you nominate in your will for the position unless that person is unavailable to act, unwilling to take on the role, or deemed unfit for the position by the court. An informal proceeding is the ideal method if it is anticipated that there will be no contest over the will or how the estate is to be handled.

On the other hand, formal probate proceedings are recommended for cases that are more complicated, have no will, or are anticipated to involve a dispute over the estate. Formal proceedings are generally filed in a similar manner as informal ones and cost the same in terms of filing fees, but this process requires different pleadings to be filed. With formal probate procedures, there will be one or more court hearings in which the probate judge will take testimony. This is why it's best to retain an experienced attorney who can professionally handle formal probate proceedings when it comes to assets, property, and estates.

HOW LONG DOES PROBATE TAKE?

This is a common question that most people ask. It really depends on several factors. For example, the size of the estate, the time it takes to validate a will, and the time it takes to notify beneficiaries can all lengthen the probate process. That being said, if there is a will and there are no complications, most probate cases take between six and nine months to complete. Once the will is filed with the probate court and a personal representative is appointed, a notice to creditors must be published in a newspaper of general circulation. After publication, creditors have 120 days to file their claims against the estate with the personal representative. This "waiting period" is for possible creditors to file their claims and is the main reason for the six- to nine-month time it takes to complete the probate proceedings. If there is no will or the will is contested, it can take even longer.

A probate can last between six and nine months, or longer, depending on several details including the size of the estate and the length of time it takes to validate a will.

HOW CAN A WILL BE CONTESTED?

Many disputes can arise during the probate process. For instance, surviving family members might not agree with the distribution of assets in the will. They might challenge the validity of the will on the basis of duress or forgery or on the mental incapacity of the decedent at the time he or she executed the will or other legal documents. There might even be disagreements over the choice of the personal representative. In all of these situations, it is wise to have a skilled elder law attorney on your side to represent you and to be your advocate when you are the estate's personal representative.

A CASE IN POINT

I was involved in litigation between siblings in a Clare County case. I was retained by a woman who lived in Arizona to challenge her stepmother's will based on a lack of testamentary capacity and undue influence from my client's half-sister, a resident of New Mexico. During litigation, I took the deposition of the deceased stepmother's primary treating doctor, and it was confirmed that when the decedent changed her will, she was already in the advanced stages of dementia. Additionally, when I took the deposition of a bank employee who had notarized a "new will" for the decedent (which had been downloaded from the Internet), the bank employee was unable to recall whether she had asked the decedent any questions that might have shed some light on the decedent's mental capacity to knowingly and intelligently understand the terms of her new will. The new will left everything to the half-sister residing in New Mexico and excluded the other half-sister who resided in Arizona (my client). My client was the daughter of the decedent's deceased husband (who, by the way, was the source of all of his widow's wealth).

The husband of the decedent had executed a similar will leaving one-half of his estate (if he survived his wife, the decedent) to each daughter (his and his wife's). After a trial, the court threw out the new will finding that the half-sister of my client had exerted undue influence over her mother and that the decedent had a lack of testamentary capacity when she executed her new will. This left the decedent's former will as the decedent's "last will and testament," and the court awarded my client approximately $200,000 that she would otherwise not have received.

If the decedent truly was of sound mind and wished to alter a previous will, she should have sought legal counsel to document her mental capacity to sign a new will and to refute any possible charges of undue influence. If such had been the case, and I had been the counsel sought out, I likely would have videotaped a discussion between myself and the client and had at least one impartial party present during such videotaping. At our meeting we would have discussed the individual's wishes, including her responses to many questions that would either support the fact that she had the mental capacity to do what she was asking or would call into question her mental capacity. If I had any doubt about her mental capacity, I would not agree to execute a new will.

That being said, if a family member suspects fraud in the inducement of making a new will or that the maker of the will lacked the testamentary capacity to know what he or she was doing or had been unduly influenced by another family member, then by all means such family member should seek legal counsel to explore the possibility of challenging any newly executed will or trust, as the case may be.

TRUST ADMINISTRATION

Trusts are administered according to the provisions contained in their terms. Generally, trusts set their own rules for administration, although there are laws that also apply. Notice to beneficiaries and creditors is required and certain actions are required fairly soon after the deceased's passing. Most often, the successor trustee carries out his or her duties with the assistance of an estate planning attorney, as well as an accountant. If the trust provides that the assets are not to be transferred to the beneficiaries for a certain period of time, for example, until they reach the age of thirty, the trust will

ATTORNEY JOSEPH T. BARBERI

operate and exist for a long time. The need for the trust will expire when there are no assets or the value of the assets is so negligible as to warrant the termination of the trust. Many trusts can be administered without court involvement, which is an advantage for people seeking privacy and avoiding family disputes. If a dispute arises, however, litigation may become necessary to resolve the issues. In addition, if a person died leaving assets, which were owned in the deceased's name alone, and not as the trustee of the trust, those assets would need to be probated. When someone signs a trust agreement as part of an estate plan, that person also creates a pour-over will, which will act to catch those assets that the individual may own in his or her name alone at the time of death and then distribute those assets to the successor trustee for distribution to the deceased's beneficiaries as set out in the trust. If this is the case, the pour-over will needs to be administered through a probate court.

CHAPTER 7

SPECIAL CIRCUMSTANCES REQUIRE SPECIAL PLANNING

TAKING CARE OF LOVED ONES WITH DISABILITIES

If you take care of someone who has a disability, one of the concerns you probably have is who will take care of your loved one if you become incapable or when you die. For those of you with children with special needs, such as autism, thinking of how to care for them after your passing can be overwhelming and daunting. In addition to having adequate life insurance, it is important to take steps to ensure that your child will be well cared for if you are incapable of doing so and when you pass away.

Fortunately, in Michigan, many children with special needs can attend school well into their twenties, which provides a care provider while parents work. Beyond that, however, the use of private care providers may become necessary, and they can be very expensive.

There are some government programs available that provide assistance to families with children with special needs. But if you die and leave a large sum of money directly to your child with special needs, it may cause your child to become disqualified from the receipt of much-needed government benefits. So, the first step to take if you have a loved one with disabilities is to ensure that you have a sufficient amount of life insurance to ensure that your loved one will be properly cared for after your passing. The second step is to consult with an experienced estate planning attorney to ensure that your estate plan is set up to provide properly for your loved one because, if done wrong, you could unwittingly deny your loved one of government benefits necessary for his or her care and well-being. In Michigan, people can establish special needs trusts to benefit a loved one with special needs. A special needs trust can be a stand-alone trust or part of a general revocable trust.

ESTATES SUBJECT TO THE FEDERAL ESTATE TAX

As of this writing, Michigan does not have an estate tax. However, the federal government imposes a federal estate tax on decedent's estates that are valued at $5,430,000 or greater in 2015. You may be thinking, I don't have $5,430,000 in assets, so I don't have to worry about federal estate taxes. But, many of us "own" assets that will be counted toward the $5,430,000, adjusted for inflation, that we don't even consider. For example, both life insurance proceeds and an interest in a business count toward the federal estate tax amount.

Married couples can take advantage of the spousal election and avoid paying hefty estate taxes by establishing a credit equivalent bypass trust, which is sometimes referred to as an A/B Trust. Per current federal tax code, assets that pass to a spouse pass tax free. In a credit bypass trust, two trusts are established. The mechanics of an A/B or credit shelter trust are beyond the scope of this book, but just be aware that it is possible to take steps to avoid or minimize federal estate taxes by the use of an A/B trust.

SECOND MARRIAGES AND BLENDED FAMILIES

Blended families face unique challenges when it comes to estate planning. The source of the problem is satisfying two competing goals for most parents in blended families: (1) taking care of their spouse and (2) taking care of their own children. Blended families are those in which one or both spouses have been married more than once, they have one or more children from a previous relationship, and they may or may not have children of their own together.

When spouses in blended families own assets jointly, the surviving spouse will own 100 percent of the asset automatically upon the death of his or her spouse. The surviving spouse will have complete control over that asset and will have no legal obligation to share any portion of that asset with anyone else, including the deceased spouse's children. If the surviving spouse remarries, he or she can transfer any or all of that asset to the new spouse or give the asset away to his or her children. The surviving spouse can sell the asset and keep 100 percent of the proceeds. Situations like these often are the source of family disputes and litigation between stepchildren and their stepparents following a parent's death.

Even when stepchildren and stepparents get along well when everyone is alive and well, emotions can run high during times of stress, such as when a loved one is sick or dying and after the loved one's death. In addition, it can be quite a shock to children to learn that their mother or father left everything to a spouse and nothing to them, not even personal items that have sentimental value to them and remind them of their childhood and time spent with their parent. Children, whether minors or adults, can feel that this kind of situation is very unfair. They are blood, and the spouse may have only known or been married to their parent for a few years. It can be even more hurtful if the surviving spouse remarries and the new spouse moves into the stepchildren's childhood home. Purchasing life insurance or providing for children and/or a spouse, allocating certain assets for a spouse and other assets for children, and/or creating a trust(s) can help provide fairly for everyone.

SAME-SEX COUPLES

The State of Michigan affords married couples certain privileges and benefits due to their marital status. One such right granted to Michigan couples is the ability to own property as tenants by the entireties. Owning property as tenants by the entireties means that the married couple owns the property as a single legal unit. The effect of this is that a creditor of one spouse may not seek payment of a debt by collecting on the married couple's real estate. Only a creditor of both spouses may do so. Another right granted to Michigan couples is the ability to inherit a share of a deceased spouse's estate under the laws of intestacy. However, contrary to popular belief, not even married couples are automatically afforded the right to make medical decisions for their spouses even if their spouses are unable to make or communicate decisions on their own behalf. Spouses are permitted to make burial arrangements after a spouse's death. Up until recently, same-sex couples in Michigan were not allowed to enjoy such benefits.

On September 21, 1996, federal legislation known as the Defense of Marriage Act, otherwise known as DOMA, was enacted. This law defined marriage as "a legal union between one man and one woman as husband and wife" and spouse as "a person of the opposite sex who is a husband or a wife." The U.S. Supreme Court held that such definitions of marriage and spouse were unconstitutional in *U.S. v. Windsor.* Thereafter, federal rights and benefits awarded to married couples were also provided to same-sex married couples. For example, same-sex couples in every state, including states such as Michigan that at that time did not recognize same-sex marriages, were afforded Social Security payments for a surviving spouse, the federal estate tax exemption provided between spouses, and the ability to file joint federal income tax returns.

Prior to the *Obergefell v. Hodges* holding by the U.S. Supreme Court on June 26, 2015, there were several provisions in Michigan law that prohibited same-sex marriages. The most notable was Section 25 of the Michigan Constitution, also known as the Marriage Amendment. It provided that a union of one man and one woman is the only agreement that will be recognized as a marriage in Michigan. There were also several Michigan statutes which provided that marriage is only between one man and one woman. Specifically, Michigan Compiled Law (MCL) 551.1 provided "[m]arriage is inherently a unique relationship between a man and a woman. As a matter of public policy, this state has a special interest in encouraging, supporting, and protecting that unique relationship in order to promote, among other goals, the stability and welfare of society and its children. A marriage contracted between individuals of the same sex is invalid in this state." In addition, MCL 551.2 also defined marriage as a "civil contract between a man and a woman." And lastly, MCL 551.3 and 4 provided that "[a] man shall not marry … another man" and "[a] woman shall not marry … another woman." These laws collectively were known as the Marriage Statutes.

These statutes have effectively been struck down by the holding in *Obergefell v. Hodges*. Same-sex couples in Michigan may marry in Michigan and their marriages entered into in other states will be recognized as legally valid in Michigan. That much is clear; what is not clear, however, is how all of the other laws, regulations, and case law in Michigan with references to husband and wife will be modified or interpreted since the *Obergefell v. Hodges* ruling.

Same-sex couples and their children should take the steps needed to affirm their legal rights as parents and children to be sure that they are allowed to exercise all of the privileges under the law provided to parents and children. Such steps may include obtaining court orders to affirm their family status. Children born to a person who is part of a same-sex marriage should now be presumed to be children of the married spouses, thereby providing legal parental status to both parents. This presumption has yet to be tested; so at this point there are no certainties to be found. A family law and estate planning attorney team, like we have at Barberi Law, can help guide you through the process of establishing and ensuring the legal role of parent and child. These roles are especially important when it comes to estate planning, as children and parents are afforded special privileges, roles, and allowances under Michigan's probate laws.

Some other implications of the *Obergefell v. Hodges* ruling is that now Michigan same-sex couples may file their state tax returns as a married couple; uncapping of property taxes should no longer occur when a member of a same-sex couple transfers real estate to his or her spouse or to a trust for his or her spouse; and same-sex couples may now enter into prenuptial and, likely, post-nuptial agreements in Michigan.

In the past, same-sex couples may have needed to take extra special care to explain their relationship in their estate planning documents to reflect their intent for their wishes should they become incapacitated and when they died. Now, often just the word "spouse" will suffice. Also, spouses are given priority over others by probate courts when it comes to appointing a guardian or conservator. In the past, because same-sex marriages were not recognized in Michigan, a same-sex spouse did not enjoy such priority. Now, same-sex couples should be given priority. Same-sex couples also receive statutory priority as spouses of those who pass without having a will. But, as always, it is better to place your wishes in writing in a will and/or trust rather than rely on statutory intestate provisions for passing on your estate. Lastly, same-sex couples can now participate in wrongful death actions and same-sex couples have an insurable interest in a deceased spouse.

WHEN GOING THROUGH A DIVORCE

When going through a divorce, there are a lot of things to think about, and one of the last things on your mind is probably your estate plan. But, the terms of your estate plan are very important and can have a profound impact on your life. If you and your spouse created and signed your estate planning documents while you were married and named each other as each other's agent, attorney-in-fact, health care advocate, co-trustee, and/or personal representative, your spouse will remain in that position until you revoke him or her from the same.

So, if you were in a coma from a car accident while you were going through a divorce and had named your spouse as your health care advocate and gave him or her the ability to remove life-sustaining treatments, your spouse would still have the power to do that even though you are going through a divorce. This is why it's wise to address the terms of your estate planning documents at the beginning of your divorce case with your divorce lawyer. Powers of attorney for medical care and finances, generally, should be reviewed and revised to remove your soon-to-be ex-spouse from any decision-making position. A new power of attorney should be considered if none was previously executed "just in case" you become disabled during the divorce process.

You may also want to review your accounts that are designated as paid on death or that are automatically transferred upon death to your spouse. In some circumstances, family court judges will issue orders, often called temporary restraining orders, which prevent either spouse from modifying or making changes to certain accounts. If such an order is in place in your divorce case, you need to work with your attorney to review and revise your estate planning documents, beneficiary designations, and accounts so that you don't violate the court's restraining order.

If you die before your minor children are eighteen years old, full custody will normally be vested in your spouse. But what if you become disabled? Use of a durable power of attorney could help you and your parents care for your minor children during a time of your disability. Upon your death, you can't assign your parenting time with your child to your new spouse or your child's grandparent. You can, however, leave a letter with your wishes and request that your child's other parent honor your wishes in the event of your death. When it comes to nominating a guardian, if you and your spouse nominate different persons for that role, the parent's nomination who dies last will typically control.

After your divorce is final, you should take steps to ensure that your estate plan is reviewed and reflects your current wishes. If you have joint accounts with your spouse or own property jointly with your spouse, you need to take steps to close joint accounts and transfer property so that you don't own anything jointly with your spouse. Some spouses wish to leave an asset or more to their former spouse, and that is fine, but it should be spelled out directly in your estate plan.

Once you are divorced, your spouse will lose the right to inherit any part of your estate through the intestacy rules of the State of Michigan. If you die during the divorce process, instead of receiving only half of the marital estate, your soon-to-be-ex spouse will receive 100 percent of the marital estate and can do with it what he or she wishes, include pass it on to his or her own children from a different relationship or to a new spouse.

If you and your spouse had one attorney draft your estate planning documents while you were married, you most likely will need to have a different attorney draft your estate planning documents pending a divorce or after a divorce. This is because your first estate planning attorney would likely have a conflict of interest if you and your spouse are going through a divorce or are divorced.

THE ROLE OF PRENUPTIAL AND POSTNUPTIAL AGREEMENTS IN ESTATE PLANNING

When most people hear the word "prenup," they think of it in the context of what happens if a married couple gets divorced. But prenuptial agreements (entered into before marriage) and postnuptial agreements (entered into after marriage) can be used as estate planning tools. Postnuptial agreements are most often entered into by people who are getting married for the second (or more) time or have a business (or one of the spouse's families has a business), or there is a significant disparity in age or wealth between the parties. Prenuptial agreements in the context of divorce are enforced by family law judges, who are oftentimes unpredictable in the way they will interpret the prenuptial agreement and whether or not they will enforce the terms of the prenuptial agreement. And, the law is ever changing regarding prenuptial agreements, so even if a couple entered into a prenuptial agreement in the 1980s, it is questionable whether it will be strictly enforced today.

In our experience, the older the prenuptial agreement is, the less likely it is that a family law judge will enforce it in the context of a divorce. When it comes to enforceability of a prenuptial agreement regarding the death of a spouse, a probate judge will be left with whether to enforce and how to interpret the terms of the prenuptial agreement. Many prenuptial agreements will leave very little to one of the spouses and will replace his or her right to statutory benefits with a life insurance policy. The purpose of a prenuptial agreement in the context of estate planning is to transfer wealth to one of the spouse's children or to protect a family business or investment. Parents may request one to prevent their child's inheritance from being shared with their child's spouse.

> Prenuptial agreements are not the most reliable form of estate planning and not the most commonly suggested tool to achieve one's goals when dealing with a second marriage or blended family or looking to protect an asset or wealth.

Prenuptial agreements must be fair at the time they are entered into; each party must fully and honestly disclose to the other well in advance of signing the prenuptial agreement of his or her assets, debts, income, and expenses. Each party should, but need not, be represented by legal counsel. It is very highly recommended that each party have an attorney and that the party who is requested to sign the prenuptial agreement have his or her own attorney thoroughly review the proposed prenuptial agreement and explain all of the terms to him or her before signing. The document should be signed well in advance of any nuptials—three to four months is ideal. Prenuptial agreements signed the day of or in the final week before the marriage are often presumed to be signed under duress or intense pressure, arguing that if the documents are not signed that the wedding will be called off. The process should be fair and the terms should be negotiated.

Postnuptial agreements are even more complex than prenuptial agreements. As is suggested by the name, postnuptial agreements are executed *after* the parties have been married. Typically, issues have arisen calling for the married couple to agree on what would happen if they should divorce, or, if one spouse dies, what would happen in regard to the disposition of marital assets or business assets owned by one or both of the parties. In such regard, the case of *Wright v. Wright,* Michigan Court of Appeals Docket #281918, decided April 22, 2008, held that postnuptial agreements were void as being against public policy. (I believe that the general principles of contract law would apply and that postnuptial agreements would be enforceable in Michigan as long as they were entered into freely and willingly by adults with equal bargaining power and with no adequate consideration being given and best accomplished with both parties being represented by counsel.) The judge and author of this Court of Appeals decision, Judge Peter D. O'Connell, has publically stated that his opinion "went too far" in, *carte blanche*, finding that postnuptial agreements should be void as against public policy.

CHAPTER 8

ESTATE PLANNING SCAMS

While most people appreciate the importance of estate planning, many are not sure how to differentiate sound advice from a sales pitch. If you are like most average adults in Michigan, you're not a financial expert and may find yourself overwhelmed by the amount of information and options available to you. An unfortunate part of estate planning is that many companies, particularly those trying to sell financial products and services, may try to take advantage of your lack of knowledge to line their pockets with your hard earned money.

> *Consulting with an estate planning attorney will help you avoid estate planning scams and dramatically reduce the stress associated with making such complex decisions.*

WHAT ARE ESTATE PLANNING SCAMS?

Estate planning scams are typically sales pitches targeting elderly citizens that use misleading tactics to collect large commission fees. The estate plans that they offer are frequently generic templates that are falsely represented and, in many cases, even legally invalid. The initiation of any con is designed to lure you in, seeming innocent and giving you no reason to suspect deceitful behavior. An estate planning scam is no different. The companies and individuals that practice these misleading sales tactics typically follow a similar script, which is presented in a few key steps. The first contact will be appealing; the "bait" is meant to attract unsuspecting targets. An invitation to a free meal is a common way to bring an audience to an informational seminar educating participants on the best practices of estate planning. This will appear to be a great opportunity to learn useful information for your financial future with the added bonus of a nice meal. The free food is just to get you in the door and to listen to a sales pitch. Information typically presented at these seminars is intentional propaganda. The presenters may be salespeople with often only one thing on their minds: commission. The supposedly nonbiased material covered will be designed to direct you to purchase the estate planning service that they provide. The aim is to convince you that their financial planning strategies are the most effective, and you are commonly not informed of any alternative methods to consider.

You may have forgotten that you gave out your contact information at the informational seminar you attended when the phone rings. The second contact is often a follow-up phone call to offer you a free exclusive in-home personalized estate planning consultation. The representative on the line may claim to be an expert who is generously willing to provide professional financial guidance to help you secure your future economic stability.

The specific language will vary slightly but the goal of the follow-up phone call is to schedule a home visit when they can seal the deal. The personalized consultation that they offer is not a unique service that you were lucky enough to be selected for. It is important to remember that the individuals who run these cons are professional salespeople, not attorneys or expert estate planners. They may make any claims or suggestions necessary to gain your trust and acquire your money.

You are often most vulnerable in your own home where you're comfortable and feel safe. This intimate environment is the ideal setting for a talented salesperson to close a deal. The visit may progress through a series of different stages in hopes of convincing you to purchase an estate plan from the company.

The beginning of your consultation will be friendly and compassionate. A savvy scammer will listen to your needs and claim to be able to customize a solution just for you. Once the salesperson establishes himself or herself as a trustworthy and knowledgeable financial advisor with expertise in estate planning, the tone may change.

The second stage is that of intimidation and scare tactics. You will be made to feel as though any previous actions you have taken toward planning your financial future have been wrong. The sales representative may suggest that your current will may not be deemed valid, your assets will be frozen, and you will lose the majority of your money to attorney fees and taxes. You might be told that your family will lose power to the court system and your beneficiaries will have to wait years after your death to receive their inheritance if anything remains of your estate.

Once you are sufficiently intimidated and obviously concerned about the long list of potential problems you have been presented with, you likely will be offered an easy solution. All you need to do to protect your money and secure your financial future is follow the representative's guidance. The salesperson may overwhelm you with the numerous benefits of a living trust with no regard for your individual situation or particular wishes. He or she will likely emphasize that you will be able to avoid probate and dramatically reduce the amount of taxes you pay out. A scammer will claim to be able to provide a fully customized estate plan drafted by a lawyer to meet your exact needs.

Once you are on the hook, you will be presented with the fine print. For a onetime fee, you can take advantage of this fail-proof strategy that will ensure economic security in your retirement years and see to it that your estate is distributed according to your wishes in the unfortunate circumstance of your demise. Now the pressure will be on to close the deal before you get any additional information or have time to change your mind. The goal is to make it seem as though the estate plan that the company can provide you is the best and only option. The con artist may tell you that this is a limited time offer and you must grab it now before it's too late. The salesperson usually insists that you take immediate action and not seek the advice of family, friends, or an attorney. The representative will typically be in a hurry to collect payment, encouraging you to simply provide your credit card number to enroll you in this once-in-a-lifetime opportunity. The truth is that there is almost always no expert or estate lawyer involved in drafting this "special" offer. The forms you will be given to sign will probably not be customized for your personal needs. They are commonly generic forms printed from a website that may or may not be accurate or even up to date. Such paperwork often does not adhere to specific state laws in Michigan or other states and can create major difficulties for your beneficiaries after your death.

Once all is said and done, if you agree to purchase an estate plan from a dishonest provider, you will be in for some surprises later on. You may find that what you agreed to was not what you thought you were signing up for. Frequently, people unwittingly fall into annuity scams. Once you pay the large fee and hand over control of your money, you discover that it is tied up in an annuity account for many years with ridiculous fees to access it early.

WHAT SHOULD YOU LOOK OUT FOR?

There are some red flags that you should keep an eye out for to help ensure you don't fall victim to an estate planning scam. It is a good rule of thumb to assume that if someone is asking for money, that person has an agenda. It is not a good idea to take a salesperson's word for anything. It is best to do your own research before making a big decision about your finances or consult an accredited expert. If an offer seems too good to be true, then trust your instincts because you are probably right. Any use of intimidation or overly aggressive sales tactics is a bad sign. You should not be pressured into making an instant decision about something as important as estate planning. If you feel uncomfortable or are discouraged from seeking outside advice, go no further. Be on the lookout for any disclaimer stating that the representative is not an estate planning attorney. This should let you know that the representative is indeed a salesperson and not an expert and, therefore, may not be a wise choice for your financial advisor.

WHAT SERVICES CAN AN ESTATE PLANNING ATTORNEY PROVIDE THAT A NON-LAWYER CAN'T?

It is in your best interest to consult with an estate planning attorney because you can be sure you are receiving accurate and unbiased information on the best options available to you. An estate planning attorney can educate you on key issues such as the pros and cons of a will versus a living trust. A lawyer will be more familiar with laws specific to Michigan to be sure you avoid any potential problems. A lawyer will also be better equipped to oversee complicated paperwork and catch any mistakes or missing information a nonprofessional could easily miss.

An estate planning attorney can advise you on a wide range of additional decisions that go along with estate planning. The lawyer can help you plan for long-term care and establish powers of attorney and is able to give you advice on Medicare, Medicaid, VA benefits, if applicable, and other special circumstances you may come across. There isn't one right answer when it comes to the most effective estate planning techniques because everyone's circumstances are different. Variables to consider range from what kind of assets you hold to who will be named as beneficiaries of your estate and many other details. Consulting with an estate planning attorney will help you avoid estate planning scams and dramatically reduce the stress associated with such complex decisions. Such consultation will allow you to be confident in your future financial security and ensure that your estate is distributed according to your final wishes.

CHAPTER 9

EIGHT ACTIONS TO TAKE RIGHT NOW TO PRESERVE YOUR WEALTH FOR YOUR FAMILY

There is no time like the present. If you don't want to be one of the thousands of people who wait too long to plan for their future and the future of their family, then start making moves today toward preserving your wealth.

Protect your wealth for your family by consulting a lawyer, separating business from personal finances, establishing liability insurances and life insurance, creating a will and a trust, utilizing retirement accounts, and understanding your pension.

1. CONSULT A LAWYER

When making any major life decisions about your assets and finances, there is often a lot of legal paperwork involved. Rather than printing a generic form from the Internet or winging it on your own, it is smarter to consult a professional who will be familiar with all of the rules and regulations of estate planning and can guide you through the process. This will help ensure that your wealth is protected and transferred to your family according to your wishes.

2. SEPARATE BUSINESS FROM PERSONAL FINANCES

If you are a business owner of any kind, it is important to separate your business finances from your personal finances. This will be beneficial to you during your lifetime and to your family when you die. Take the necessary steps to create a corporation or limited liability company that can protect your family's money or property in the event of business problems, bankruptcy, or liability claims.

3. ESTABLISH LIABILITY INSURANCES

If you want to protect your wealth, you should have insurance coverage across the board. Whether it is homeowners, auto, health, long-term care, or business insurance, if you don't have it to protect you from unexpected circumstances, your money could practically disappear overnight. If you have high value assets, it is often prudent to invest in an umbrella policy that will cover above and beyond the normal payout of your other insurances in case of emergency. No matter how smart you are or how well you manage your money, a lawsuit, serious illness, or accident can undo years of financial planning without insurance to help compensate your expenses.

4. SET UP LIFE INSURANCE

Life insurance is a separate legal contract set up between you and your insurance company in addition to your estate plan. This means that in the event of your death, your life insurance policy will be paid out directly and generally does not have to go through probate court to be distributed. When you set up your policy, select your beneficiary carefully and pay attention to the manner in which it will be paid out. Properly drafted beneficiary designations for your life insurance proceeds can ensure that such proceeds will be protected for the benefit of your trust beneficiaries and avoid probate.

5. CREATE A WILL

One of the first logical steps in planning your estate and protecting your assets for your family is creating a will. In a will, you can specify important wishes such as how to distribute your assets, name your beneficiaries, and nominate a guardian for your children, as well as other critical matters that should be documented. Consult with your lawyer and get the ball rolling to draft a will today.

6. UTILIZE RETIREMENT ACCOUNTS

Retirement accounts are a good way to invest in your future financial stability and that of your family. In many cases these accounts are protected from bankruptcy in the event of financial hardship, so they are a safe place to put away your money to access later on.

7. UNDERSTAND YOUR PENSION

Familiarize yourself with how your pension plan is set up and clarify your nomination of beneficiary(ies) and how your survivor benefit will be paid out. Just like a life insurance payout, these details may be easy to overlook now but will become important in the future. This is another instance in which it would be wise to set up your payment to be entered into a trust account to protect the recipient from excess tax penalties.

8. CREATE A TRUST

Placing some of you money or other assets into a trust is an excellent way to protect your assets and pass them on to your loved ones. In this arrangement, your designated assets are held by a third party, called a trustee, to be distributed to the beneficiaries according to your wishes. You can set up a trust to be paid out at a certain age, in set amounts, or in any manner that you see fit. A trust does not have to go through probate. Not only will the money or assets be protected and separate from the rest of your estate but also your beneficiaries will not be penalized for receiving distribution from your trust.

CHAPTER 10

RESOURCES

In addition to the information in this book, other sources of information are available to help keep you up to date on changes in the law. I have listed resources that serve people interested in estate planning.

BARBERI LAW FREE ESTATE PLANNING AND ASSET PROTECTION WORKSHOPS

You are welcome to attend one of our free Estate Planning and Asset Protection Workshops, which are held twice monthly, typically on either a Tuesday or Wednesday, starting at 5:30 p.m. To reserve your spot at the next seminar, please call our office at (989) 773-3423. At the time of this writing, seminar attendees also receive a free, one-on-one consultation with an experienced estate planning attorney that will be scheduled for a later date and time at your convenience.

BARBERI LAW MONTHLY NEWSLETTER

Each month we provide our readers with valuable and useful information about the law, our Mid-Michigan community, and more. When changes are made to the law and regulations that may affect you and your family, we let you know. To sign up to receive our newsletter, contact us through our website at BarberiLawFirm.com or e-mail us at Admin@BarberiLawFirm.com. Or you may wish to call us at (989) 773-3423 or write to us at Barberi Law, 2305 Hawthorn Drive, Ste C, Mt. Pleasant, Michigan, 48858.

FIVE WISHES

This is a national program facilitated by the group Aging with Dignity and it provides senior citizens with an easy-to-follow process for discussing medical care at the end of their lives. If you are not able to consult with an attorney regarding a medical power of attorney, this is a resource you should consider utilizing. The program is called Five Wishes because it focuses on five questions that will build the foundation of an advance directive to communicate with doctors and loved ones regarding how you would like to be cared for later in life. You can easily fill out the forms online and personalize your document to your needs in a matter of minutes. Learn more about the program at www.agingwithdignity.org/five-wishes. php or give Five Wishes a call toll free at (888) 5Wishes (594-7437). You can also send an e-mail to fivewishes@ agingwithdignity.com or fill out a contact form on the website.

ISABELLA COUNTY COMMISSION ON AGING

Established in 1973, this organization provides elderly citizens and their families with resources for care services and engaging activities in the area. Some of the direct care services offered are homemaking, transportation, and a senior companion program. When it comes to activities, this organization has created various programs to get senior citizens involved, such as a volunteer program, a foster grandparent program, and other similar groups. The organization's website can be found at www. isabellacounty.org/dept/coa, where there is also a directory with contact information for specific departments.

SENIOR SERVICES OF MIDLAND COUNTY

This organization provides elderly citizens and their families with resources for care services and engaging activities in the area. Some of the direct care services offered are meals on wheels, counseling, memory support services, and health benefits. When it comes to activities, this organization has created various programs to get senior citizens involved with activity centers located in Coleman, Greendale, and Sanford. The organization's website can be found at www.seniorservices.midland.org, where there is also a directory with contact information for specific departments.

AMERICAN ASSOCIATION OF RETIRED PERSONS (AARP):

AARP is one of the most popular national nonprofit organizations that strives to protect the rights of senior citizens all over the country. You have to be a member to obtain discounts and special services, but it's rather easy to join. Its current membership is estimated to be more than 37 million and it has offices in all fifty states. Visit the website at www.aarp.org/ or contact AARP directly toll free at 1-888-OUR-AARP (1-888-687-2277).

ASSOCIATION OF MATURE AMERICAN CITIZENS (AMAC):

This group is similar to AARP, but it is a newer organization and has fewer members. AMAC most commonly puts together committees to share the perspective of elderly persons with members of Congress and other forms of government. If you would like more information, visit the website at www.amac.us/ or call 1-888-262-2006.

SENIOR TIMES OF SOUTH CENTRAL MICHIGAN

Usually just referred to as *Senior Times*, this magazine is a local publication intended for senior citizen readers in the south central Michigan area. The monthly publication features stories and articles to provide elderly residents with information applicable to them. You can download issues at www.scenepub.com/seniortimes, call (269) 979-1410, or e-mail ssherban@wwthayne.com for more information.

HOSPICE AND PALLIATIVE CARE ASSOCIATION OF MICHIGAN

This organization is dedicated to providing senior citizens of Michigan with education regarding options, advance care planning resources, and support. Founded in 1979, the organization has long been trusted as one of the best long-term medical care resources for the elderly in Michigan. There is a place on its website (**www.mihospice.org**) where you can fill out a contact form to receive more information about its services.

MICHIGAN FUNERAL DIRECTORS ASSOCIATION (MFDA)

This association was founded in 1880 and is considered to be the oldest organization of funeral professionals in the United States. The MFDA is a private professional association consisting of approximately 1,300 funeral directors from Michigan who work to ensure the very best quality of funeral services in the area. Visit their website at **www.mfda.org** to learn more, call (517) 349-9565, or e-mail info@mfda.org.

AREA AGENCIES ON AGING (AAAS)

AAA is an organization devoted to building a collective voice to provide senior citizens with the education necessary to ensure healthy aging while maintaining their dignity and independence. The AAA Association of Michigan is located at 6105 W. St. Joseph Hwy, Suite 204, Lansing, Michigan, 48917. You can also visit the website at **www.mi-seniors.net** or call (517) 886-1029.

GET WHAT'S YOURS - THE SECRET TO MAXING OUT YOUR SOCIAL SECURITY

by Laurence J. Kotlikoff and Philip Moeller. As discussed in this book, the authors of *Get What's Yours* describe methods for maxing out your Social Security benefits—methods that are not well known and openly shared by the Social Security Administration.

CHAPTER 11

EPILOGUE

This book was written to raise the consciousness of Michigan citizens as to their options when formulating their unique estate plans. All too often people think of estate plans as dreary, life-ending documents that "have to be done" when people get very old and begin to confront end-of-life decisions due to their declining health. Nothing could be farther from the truth.

I regularly speak to high school students in death and dying classes about the importance of making estate plans when they graduate from high school. Young people do get married and have children, and tragedies happen, which either cause an early disability or an untimely death, leaving young children and a widow or widower behind. And tragically, sometimes both a young father and mother die in the same car accident leaving the probate court to decide who should care for their young children because neither parent had written down their intentions and wishes. Recalling my previous reference to Terri Schiavo in Chapter 1 regarding powers of attorney, Terri was only twenty-six years of age when she became incapacitated. Young people need wills and need to have their preferences known when it comes to whom they would choose for guardians and/or conservators for their children should something happen to them.

I hope I have made it abundantly clear that the worst mistake individuals can make (no matter how intelligent and how well read they might be) is to engage in their own estate planning (DIY) without the advice of an experienced estate planning attorney. My message has nothing to do with increasing the financial income of attorneys who regularly engage in estate planning, but everything to do with making sure that what an individual wants to have happen does, in fact, happen, especially regarding his or her personal care during any period of disability and where the individual's assets go after death. Recall my Chapter 4 reference to the father of my Texas client, who titled $1.4 million to my client's half-sister and whose plan for destiny failed (she would do the right thing, wouldn't she?).

I hope the reader has also learned that the important decisions that go with creating a person's estate plan should be made at a time when health issues are not confronting the individual. After such an initial plan is in place, the individual is then encouraged to revisit and consider modifying his or her estate plan every three to five years as the individual's life progresses, based on any new issues that might develop.

In closing, even if you or your spouse have previously had an attorney draft a will or a will and a trust for you, it may be time to review such documents with an experienced elder law attorney. The lawyer can help you decide if there are reasons to revise and amend your and/or your spouse's previous estate plan. This type of review is especially important if you and your spouse are involved in a second marriage. And, remember that acquiring knowledge begins the path to wisdom.

HOW TO SUBSCRIBE TO OUR NEWSLETTER OR GET IT SENT TO A FRIEND OR FAMILY MEMBER

If you are reading this book, you might also be receiving our monthly hard copy newsletter, *The Barberi Law Insider*. Our newsletter covers interesting stories about the law, news items that we believe you will find very useful and interesting, and other information to keep you up to date on relevant changes in Michigan's laws.

If you would like to recommend family and/or friends who you believe might also be interested in receiving *The Barberi Law Insider*, simply provide us with their names and addresses. We would be delighted to reach more interested individuals. We'll send each of them our monthly newsletter, along with a note telling them that you graciously referred them. Don't worry, we don't spam nor do we share information with any other parties. (If, for any reason, they don't want to receive it, there is always a toll-free number that they can call to remove a name from the subscription list.)

If you are *not* receiving our newsletter and would like to, we'll be happy to sign you up for a free subscription.

SUBSCRIBING IS EASY

Call with names and addresses (and e-mail addresses if available) or send requests via fax, e-mail, or standard mail.

Call: 989-773-3423
E-mail: admin@barberilawfirm.com
Fax: 989-772-6444

Mail:
Barberi Law
2305 Hawthorn Drive, Ste. C,
Mt. Pleasant, MI 48858

We also have an e-mail version of our monthly newsletter, and if you would prefer to receive your copy in your in-box, simply provide us with your e-mail address.

HOW TO GET ANOTHER COPY OF THIS BOOK

If others want a free copy of this book, or you want an additional copy to give to a friend, fill out the form below and mail it to us, or simply send us a note with the names and addresses of the people you think would appreciate a free copy. We will promptly put one in the mail. We also have an e-book version that we can send via e-mail.

If confidentiality is an issue, you can pick up a copy from one of our law offices:

Barberi Law
2305 Hawthorn Drive, Suite C
Mt. Pleasant, MI 48858

Barberi Law
1618 Denver Road
Midland, MI 48640

Copies can also be ordered at Amazon.com, but there is a $17.95 sales price.

☑ **YES PLEASE SEND ME A FREE COPY OF MR. BARBERI'S BOOK!**
ESTATE PLANNING in MICHIGAN

Name: _____
Address: _____
City: _____ State: _____ Zip: _____
E-mail address: _____

☐ *Please check this box if you would like the e-book version.*

We appreciate your referrals and thank you in advance for your confidence in Barberi Law.

IMPORTANT DISCLAIMER

This is an informational consumer guide intended to assist the public. It is not legal or financial advice. Laws change; court decisions interpreting and changing case precedent occur weekly; all of these changes can cause advice to change as well, even advice based on the same facts. Some observant readers may come across a fact or two that might appear to be in error. They may consider writing me to point out such observations. In our world, my advice is we should all try to save trees (paper). There are mistakes in this book, as with most books. No matter how hard one tries to avoid mistakes, they will always occur. My hope is that such unintended errors will be insignificant in nature and that those observant readers finding errors will be both understanding and forgiving.

Accordingly, comments and opinions set forth in this book should not be relied on as legal advice or professional advice of any kind. Reading this book does not create an attorney/client relationship between the author and the reader. To receive proper legal advice or professional advice of any kind, an individual needs to discuss his or her unique facts with professionals who, at that time, will then be in a position to give the client their best professional advice.

ABOUT THE AUTHOR

Mr. Barberi has practiced law in the Central Michigan area for over thirty years. For twelve years, Mr. Barberi served as Prosecuting Attorney for Isabella County. Mr. Barberi is a graduate of Central Michigan University and a cum laude graduate of the Detroit College of Law, which is now Michigan State University College of Law. Mr. Barberi ranked fifth in his graduating class of 241 students.

For over twenty-five years, Mr. Barberi has been a member of the Probate and Estate Planning Law Section of the Michigan State Bar. Mr. Barberi has been recognized by his peers, having been appointed by the Michigan Supreme Court to serve on a committee revising Michigan's Rules of Court. While serving as Prosecuting Attorney for Isabella County, he was elected by his fellow Michigan prosecutors to serve as their

President of the Prosecuting Attorneys Association of Michigan (PAAM).

In 2007 and 2008 Mr. Barberi attended national symposiums in Atlanta, Georgia, and Hartford, New York, with Medicaid Practice Systems to become certified to assist Medicaid applicants in qualifying for the payment of their nursing home care. Thereafter, Mr. Barberi began conducting monthly workshops in the central Michigan area, traveling to Greenville, Alma, and Midland, as well as Mount Pleasant. As a result of these workshops, more than 1,000 individuals have been exposed to strategies to help their families protect assets from today's staggering high costs of nursing home care.

Mr. Barberi is also a past president of the Isabella County Bar Association. Readers of Central Michigan University's (*CM Life*) newspaper have voted Mr. Barberi their #1 attorney for fourteen years in a row. Readers of the *Morning Sun* newspaper have voted Mr. Barberi as their #1 attorney in the Central Michigan area for fifteen years in a row.

BARBERI LAW

EVERY CASE WE TAKE,
WE TAKE PERSONALLY.®

2305 Hawthorn Drive, Ste C,
Mt. Pleasant, MI 48858

1-800-336-3423
www.BarberiLawFirm.com

WA